D0301385

Trump, the Alt-Right and Public Pedagogies of Hate and for Fascism

Trump, the Alt-Right and Public Pedagogies of Hate and for Fascism: What Is To Be Done? uses public pedagogy as a theoretical lens through which to view discourses of hate and for fascism in the era of Trump and to promote an anti-fascist and pro-socialist public pedagogy. It makes the case for re-igniting a rhetoric that goes beyond the undermining of neoliberal capitalism and the promotion of social justice, and re-aligns the left against fascism and for a socialism of the twenty-first century.

Beginning with an examination of the history of traditional fascism in the twentieth century, the book looks at the similarities and differences between the Trump regime and traditional Western post-war fascism. Cole goes on to consider the alt-right movement, the reasons for its rise, and the significance of the internet being harnessed as a tool with which to promote a fascist public pedagogy. Finally, the book examines the resistance against these discourses and addresses the question of: what is to be done?

This topical book will be of great interest to scholars, to postgraduate students and to researchers, as well as to advanced undergraduate students in the fields of education studies, pedagogy, politics, and sociology, as well as readers in general who are interested in the phenomenon of Trumpism.

Mike Cole is Professor in Education in the International Centre for Public Pedagogy at the University of East London.

This is an excellent book – it's a highly engaging read that will be of interest to people who don't already know a great deal about Trump and the alt-right and the various movements who oppose them, as well as those who are already well-versed in the horrors of Trumpism. The book makes good use of public pedagogy as a framing device, and it will be an important contribution to our further understanding of how dominant ideologies are enacted and perpetuated, and also how they are resisted.

Jennifer Sandlin
Editor of the *Journal of Curriculum and Pedagogy*, co-author of 'Mapping the Complexity of Public Pedagogy Scholarship 1894–2010' and co-editor of the *Handbook of Public Pedagogy*
School of Social Transformation, Arizona State University, Tempe AZ

Trump, the Alt-Right and Public Pedagogies of Hate and for Fascism

What Is To Be Done?

Mike Cole

Routledge
Taylor & Francis Group

LONDON AND NEW YORK

First published 2019
by Routledge
2 Park Square, Milton Park, Abingdon, Oxon OX14 4RN

and by Routledge
52 Vanderbilt Avenue, New York, NY 10017

Routledge is an imprint of the Taylor & Francis Group, an informa business

© 2019 Mike Cole

British Library Cataloguing-in-Publication Data
A catalogue record for this book is available from the British Library

Library of Congress Cataloging-in-Publication Data
A catalog record for this book has been requested

ISBN: 978-1-138-60754-5 (hbk)
ISBN: 978-0-429-46714-1 (ebk)

Typeset in Times New Roman
by Apex CoVantage, LLC

MIX
Paper from
responsible sources
FSC
www.fsc.org   FSC® C013985

Printed in the United Kingdom
by Henry Ling Limited

Contents

Acknowledgments

I would like to thank Shane Burley, Sal Chambers, Antonia Darder, Derek Ford, Rich Gibson, Dave Hill, Vinnie Kidd, Curry Malott, Peter McLaren, Glenn Rikowski, Sue Wilkins, and Faith Agostinone Wilson for their constructive comments on this book. Special thanks to Alpesh Maisuria for making helpful comments on a whole draft of an earlier version of the book, and to Jennifer Sandlin for her characteristic insightful comments on public pedagogy scholarship addressed in the book, in a later version. The presence here of the aforementioned scholars, activists, and friends does not necessarily imply agreement with all the content of the book and, of course, any inadequacies in the analysis remain mine.

Introduction

Public pedagogy

Trump becomes president

In the early hours of the morning on November 9, 2016, the unthinkable became reality – a ruthless, sociopathic, racist, misogynist, disablist, climate-change denying[1] real estate mogul and reality TV star became the first billionaire president of the United States of America.[2] His predecessor, the country's first black president (whose US citizenship Trump has questioned), whatever his public pedagogy – most notably 'yes we can'[3] – and his real intentions or beliefs, had done little to curb capitalism's excesses. Instead, in part on account of the structural constraints of the office of president (Friedman, 2017), he found himself reinforcing neoliberal capitalism's aggressive and destructive policies, while continuing to bolster US imperialist hegemony. The election of Donald J. Trump, however, denoted a quantum leap in the degeneracy of (especially American) capitalism and, even more frighteningly, represented a massive lurch in the direction of fascism, as argued throughout this book. As the truth sank in, and as the revelations of his support base emerged gradually over the coming days and weeks, it became clear that the far-right forces surrounding Trump had an academic core accompanying the allegiance of sections of the ruling class and the dispossessed that is always a primary feature of fascist and fascistic movements: hence the need for an academic response, of which this book forms a part. Reading a large amount of material on Trump, and on the alternative right – the alt-right – revealed how and the ways in which *public pedagogy* facilitates the spread of hate and of far right ideology.

Public pedagogy

I first encountered the concept of public pedagogy when I joined the International Centre for Public Pedagogy (ICPUP, 2018) at the University of

East London on May 1, 2013. This discovery was a revelation to me because after decades of involvement in using and writing about traditional institutional pedagogy to promote equality (e.g. Cole, 1989, 2009, 2011a, 2018) (I did use public pedagogy at the same time, but was not aware that I was using it) I was always of the opinion that pedagogy could and should play a wider role than its institutional one. Given the forcefulness, the incessant regularity, the rage, fervor, and high degree of fanaticism of Trump's attempts to communicate his views, he is self-evidently engaged in a form of public pedagogy. This serves not only as an attempt to 'educate' the public at large, often to promote racism, sexism, and climate change misinformation, and, on one occasion, to mock disability, but also to embolden and legitimize the views of individuals and groups with core fascist beliefs. One such group, the alt-right, also heavily involved in public pedagogy, is the subject of chapters 3 and 4 of this book.

At this point, it is necessary to briefly consider the precise meaning of the concept of 'public pedagogy'. As social justice educator Roger Simon (1995, 109) has argued, pedagogy as a concept lends itself to a multiplicity of sites for education to take place, which are 'multiple, shifting and overlapping'. The concept of *public* pedagogy has been defined by Jennifer Sandlin and her colleagues simply as 'educational activity and learning in extrainstitutional spaces and discourses' (Sandlin et al., 2011, 338).[4] Public pedagogy, they go on:

> has been largely constructed as a concept focusing on various forms, processes, and sites of education and learning occurring beyond formal schooling and is distinct from hidden and explicit curricula operating within and through school sites.[5]
>
> (Sandlin et al., 2011, 338–339)

'Public pedagogy' has appeared in academic literature since 1894, but its presence has only been significant since the end of the twentieth century, having greatly increased since 2006 (Sandlin et al., 2011, Figure 1, p. 341). One of its foremost advocates, Henry Giroux, commends the work of David Trend (1992), Roger Simon (e.g. 1992, 1995) and others for extending pedagogy's 'application far beyond the classroom while also attempting to combine the cultural and the pedagogical as part of a broader vision of political education and cultural studies' (Giroux, 2004, 61).[6] As Sandlin et al. (2010) explain, public pedagogy involves learning in educational sites such as popular culture, media, commercial spaces and the internet; and through figures and sites of activism, including public intellectuals and grassroots social movements. In addition, Donna Kerr (1999) locates pedagogy within the act of public speech itself. Public pedagogy scholars thus pose a multidimensional understanding of public education in democratic societies and relate it to 'the development of the ideological social-political nation within the consciousness and lived practices of that nation's citizenry' (Sandlin et al., 2011, 342).

As we shall see in this chapter and in chapters 2, 3, and 4, Trump and the alt-right make full use of the various public pedagogy sites. Unlike the public pedagogy of Trump and the alt-right, the overwhelming focus of the majority of historical and contemporary public pedagogy theorists is on the promotion of social justice for all. To this end, as Sandlin et al. (2011) point out, many have been involved in a counter-hegemonic project against neoliberal capitalism and its multiple manifestations *per se*, and/or against the oppression of multiple identities, such as gender, 'race', age, sexual orientation, and social class that it upholds. Moreover, although 'the context and meaning of [public pedagogy] differ[s] in early sources from current parlance, in some ways the general axiological import remains consistent – the term in its earliest usage [dating back to 1894] implied a form of educational discourse in the service of the *public good*' (Sandlin et al., 2011, 341–342). A central contribution to public pedagogy has been from feminist scholars, who have argued that the teaching and learning inherent in everyday life can be both oppressive and resistant (Sandlin et al., 2011, 344). As I will demonstrate, the public pedagogies and actions of Donald Trump and the alt-right reinforce the very forms of oppression that public pedagogy has traditionally challenged and aim to undermine gains made by promoters of social justice over decades, if not centuries of struggle.

Given the historical emphasis of public pedagogy on social justice and the common good, it might at first appear difficult to transpose such progressive efforts of critical educators within public pedagogy on to the deeply reactionary project of Trump and the alt-right, whose joint aims are less equality and less social justice. However, given that Trump and the alt-right are also clearly and manifestly engaged in public pedagogy *against* the perceived liberalism of the Democratic Party and, openly with respect to the alt-right, *for* 'white supremacy' and a white ethno-state, then there is an urgent need to attempt this theoretical transition. Sandlin et al. (2011, 363) make the case for 'increased efforts by researchers, activists, artists, and practitioners to take up questions around educations that exist outside of institutional purview', stressing the need to address 'decentred sites of resistance . . . and . . . the species of pedagogy occurring in public spaces that might still elude our vision' (Sandlin et al., 2011, 364). The public pedagogies of Trump and the alt-right are two such sites and two such public spaces that have not been comprehensively analyzed within public pedagogy literature. Just as Giroux (1998, 2000), in Sandlin et al.'s (2011, 344) words, is 'collectively subverting dominant ideologies', so are Trump and the alt-right, but from the perspective of the radical right rather than from the left. Whereas public pedagogy has traditionally been *for* more social justice and more equality, that of Trump and the alt-right is, to repeat, from a progressive perspective, for less justice and equality.[7]

How then to begin a public pedagogy analysis of Trump and the alt-right? Public pedagogy analysis has been deployed to look at ways in which oppressive discourses are permeated. Pertinent to the concerns of this book, Giroux (2010, 7) refers to a 'public pedagogy of hate' emitted out by a 'right-wing spin machine', influenced by the US right-wing media, in particular conservative radio talk show hosts, that 'endlessly spews out a toxic rhetoric' against Muslims, African Americans and other people of color, immigrants, and many other groups (Giroux, 2010, 8). In the chapters of this book, I draw on, extend, and develop Giroux's concept in an attempt to understand the public pedagogies of both Trump and the alt-right, and also introduce new public pedagogy formulations.

Outline of the book

Before I outline the chapters, it should be pointed out that the focus of this book is the effect of Trump and the alt-right on the American people, and the threat they pose to (working class) people of color by the promotion and escalation of racism via public pedagogy and policy initiatives, and to the working class *per se* by the (attempted) move of fascism towards the mainstream, a shift that all progressive people ignore at our peril. The book should not be seen as diminishing or undermining the significance of pre-Trump and non-Trump related conditions of working class people, of the poor, and of the institutional racism that is endemic in US society. I deal with inequality and (racialized and gendered) poverty in the first section, 'Reality' of chapter 5 of this book, and with racialized capitalism in the US historically and contemporaneously at length elsewhere (e.g. Cole, 2011b, chapter 3, 2016, chapter 2, 2017a, chapter 6).

The subject matter of chapter 1 is Trump himself. In order to assess claims that Trump is a fascist, I begin the chapter with a brief consideration of Trump and traditional fascism as it existed in the first four decades of the twentieth century, after which it ceased to be a hegemonic force following World War II. I then attempt to identify some key features of fascism, based primarily on the works of Michael Mann and Dave Renton (the latter's preferred formulation having been derived from the writings and activism of Leon Trotsky). In the light of this analysis of fascism, I move on to my own particular response to a question consistently and constantly posed since the ascendancy of Trump: 'is Trump a (neo-) fascist'? In the course of the discussion, in addition to Trump's relationship to pre-war fascism, I also consider his sexism and his disablism. Given the crisis of climate change and Trump's denial of it, I conclude with a discussion of the implications of such a rebuttal with respect to the inter-relationship between fascism and the very survival of our planet – in Carl Beijer's words, fascism's pincer: on the one side, looming ecological catastrophe and economic pathology coupled with scapegoating immigrants and, on the other, ethnonationalism, the alt-right and fascism.

In the first part of chapter 2, I begin with a consideration of Trump's racist and fascistic rhetoric in his speeches, a key feature of his public pedagogy platform, and the accompanying agenda, targeted at Mexicans and others living in the US or wanting to cross the US border; and at Muslims. I go on to document his condescending and racist references to Native Americans. In this section of the chapter, I also address Trump's alleged derogatory remarks about African Americans and people from Africa and Haiti. I then consider in some detail Trump and the DACA program. In the second part of chapter 2, I concentrate on the president's use of Twitter, his use of tweets and retweets to bring political public pedagogy directly to the public in order to promote a public pedagogy of hate and to add legitimacy to fascism. I argue, following Brian Ott, that Twitter is defined by three key features: simplicity, impulsivity, and incivility, and that these coincide with Trump's persona.

The alt-right is the subject matter of chapters 3 and 4. In chapter 3, I first of all consider the political and economic backdrop that has led to the ascendancy of Trump and the growth of fascism. I move on to analyze the rhetoric and agenda of the alt-right, focusing on some key alt-right figures, including Richard Spencer and Andrew Anglin. With respect to the latter, I pay particular emphasis on that neo-Nazi's history of the alt-right movement and his interpretation of what the alt-right is all about. I conclude the chapter with a brief look at alt-right activist Christopher Cantwell, and his public pedagogy for fascism, which, as is the case for some other key alt-right figures, takes place on the streets and via the internet.

Chapter 4's purpose is a specific examination of the internet as used by the alt-right to promote a public pedagogy for fascism. I look at three major alt-right organs of public pedagogy, a Reddit (an American social news aggregation) known as The_Donald, used by five groups with various key interests, but composed of disaffected white men who share a common hatred of social justice and an admiration for Trump; the National Policy Institute, which is calling for policy initiatives in preparation for its goal of a fascist America; and a key article that appears on the US alt-right website, also a call for action for a fascist future. Hopefully, chapters 3 and 4 will serve as a wake-up call. The most disturbing aspect of preparing this book was that, despite all the alleged 'jokes' and the so-called self-styled macabre and sickening 'humor' – 'only joking' – that characterizes the alt-right, the movement is serious about creating fascism and is working on ways to try to achieve it. Here I would like to stress that I have tried to get the balance right between warning of the real dangers of fascism becoming more mainstream, while at the same time not underestimating the importance, and indeed successes of movements, forces, and the various groupings that oppose fascism and have different visions of the future of America. Hopefully, I have not overestimated the significance of the alt-right. With this in mind, the book should be considered as a whole, with the two remaining chapters given equal weight to the preceding four.

Thus, having concentrated on the public pedagogy and policies of Trump and the alt-right in the first four chapters, in chapters 5 and 6, I address the issue of what is to be done. In chapter 5, I turn my attention to resistance to both Trump and the alt-right, but first I consider the reality of capitalism in the US in 2018, with respect to both inequality and poverty. I then examine the actuality, as opposed to the rhetoric, of Donald Trump in a self-explanatory section of the chapter entitled 'Trump against the US working class'. Moving on to resistance, I sketch the multiple protests against Trump that have taken place since the announcement of his candidacy up to the time of writing this book. In the following section of chapter 5, I assess the success of Antifa (the main US anti-fascist movement) in seriously undermining the project of the alt-right, before concluding with a consideration of public pedagogy against fascism, including the issue of 'no platform for fascists'.

In the final chapter of the book, chapter 6, the main focus is a public pedagogy for socialism as an antidote to Trump and the alt-right, and as a positive vision for the future. I begin the chapter with a look at some socialistic movements prominent in the US, followed by two women's movements; Black Lives Matter; and the ANSWER Coalition (Act Now to Stop War and End Racism). Next I consider two socialist groupings and some socialist parties. I conclude the chapter and the book with some suggestions, based on previous analysis, as to what a United Socialist States of America might look like and, given the hegemony of (neoliberal) capitalism, whether such a vision is possible. As well as epitomizing the essential features of non-Stalinist socialism, a socialism for and of the twenty-first century must be fully inclusive, embracing all social justice issues and it must centralize ecological imperatives.

Notes

1 That Trump is a sociopath is also the view of Dr Lance Dodes, a former assistant professor of clinical psychiatry at Harvard Medical School who now works for the Boston Psychoanalytic Society and Institute (Kentish, 2017a). Trump's racism, misogyny, disablism, and climate change denial are all dealt with in this book.

2 Trump's rise in real estate in the 1970s; his casino-fuelled stardom in the 1980s; his near financial ruin in the 1990s; and his political ambitions and reality show stardom in the two decades leading up to his presidency (Michel, 2018) are dealt with in an excellent insightful four-part series, *Trump: An American Dream* (Netflix) that paints a picture of Trump that coincides with many of the observations in this book of the Trump persona.

3 For the full text of Obama's victory speech, see *The Independent* (2008).

4 It is outside my scope in this book to discuss pedagogy in its traditional institutional usage. For analyses of the history and application of the concept of pedagogy in this sense, see, for example, Smith (2012); Brühlmeier (2010); Smith and Smith (2008); Hamilton (1999).

5 Sandlin et al. are using 'school' and 'schooling' in their US sense to encompass all institutional education, not just pre-college, pre-university schools, as in the UK convention.

6 For a comprehensive edited collection on public pedagogy, comprising some 65 chapters, see Sandlin et al., (eds) 2010 and for an exhaustive overview of 420 sources, see Sandlin et al. (2011).

7 Trump and the alt right argue, as we shall see, that their agenda is social justice for (working class) white men and for the rich who have lived and been successful in the American Dream that they believe rewards hard work.

1 'One glorious destiny in one shared home that belongs to us'

The ominous rise of Donald J. Trump

Introduction

In this first chapter, I begin my making some brief comments about Donald Trump and fascism, before going to identify some of fascism's key features, both as a set of significant ideas and as a dialectic of reactionary ideology and mass movement. Having analyzed fascism, I go on to assess the extent to which Trump himself may be considered a fascist. In the course of this discussion, I address not just the far-right and Trump's relation to it, but also the issues of sexism and disability. After this, I turn my attention to Trump's position on climate change in late capitalism, and Carl Beijer's concept of fascism's pincer.

President Donald J. Trump and fascism

John Broich (2016) poses the following questions:

> How to cover the rise of a political leader who's left a paper trail of anti-constitutionalism, racism and the encouragement of violence? Does the press take the position that its subject acts outside the norms of society? Or does it take the position that someone who wins a fair election is by definition 'normal', because his leadership reflects the will of the people?

Broich is not referring to the election of Donald J. Trump. These are, in fact, the questions that confronted the US press after the ascendance of fascist leaders in Italy and Germany in the 1920s and 1930s. In 1939, in a speech to the Reichstag, Adolph Hitler stated:

> If the international Jewish financiers . . . succeed in plunging the nations once more into a world war, then the results will . . . be . . . the annihilation of the Jewish race in Europe.
>
> (US Government Print Office,
> 1949–1953, Vol X111, 131)

Nearly eight decades later, at the United Nations (central mission: the maintenance of international peace and security) Trump warned:

> North Korea . . . threatens the entire world with unthinkable loss of human life . . . The United States . . . if it is forced to defend itself or its allies . . . will have no choice but to totally destroy North Korea.
>
> (Politico Staff, 2017)[1]

These two quotes are more or less identical, apart from the constituency under threat in each. In addition, one can substitute 'North Korea' for 'Iran', or any other future country that attracts the President's ire.

A willingness to unleash mass violence, unfortunately, may not be the only trait that Hitler and Trump have in common. Historical significance may be another factor. Those who dismiss Trump as a temporary aberration, or of no lasting consequence, might well take note of Broich's (2016) vignette concerning American journalist Dorothy Thompson. In 1928, Thompson described Hitler as a man of 'startling insignificance'. Realizing her mistake in 1935 (she had met Hitler in 1931), she declared:

> No people ever recognize their dictator in advance. He never stands for election on the platform of dictatorship. He always represents himself as the instrument [of] the Incorporated National Will.
>
> (Thompson, 1935, cited in Broich, 2016)

Referring to the US, Thompson (1935) went on, 'When our dictator turns up you can depend on it that he will be one of the boys, and he will stand for everything traditionally American' (cited in Broich, 2016). Trump certainly wants *to appear to be* 'one of the boys', his boasting about sexual assault and dismissing it as 'locker room talk' (Gregory, 2016), being a prime example.[2] As far as being 'traditionally American' is concerned, as Libby Hill (2017) points out, despite Trump and rapper Kanye West having had a high-profile meeting at Trump Tower in December 2016, sparking speculation that West might end up participating in the inauguration celebration, the Presidential Inaugural Committee chairman Tom Barrack stated in an interview with CNN:

> [w]e haven't asked him. He considers himself a friend of the president-elect, but it's not the venue. The venue we have for entertainment is filled out. It's perfect. It's going to be typically and traditionally American, and Kanye is a great guy, we just haven't asked him to perform. We move on with our agenda.
>
> (cited in Hill, 2017)

Traditional America in Trump's dreams probably consists of a white able-bodied heterosexual 'all-American' couple in a diner eating apple pie, before going to the drive-in movie in their old Buick, to watch John Wayne (of English, Ulster-Scots, and Irish ancestry) in *Blood Alley*, in which Wayne stars as Captain Tom Wilder, an American Merchant Marine, whose ship is seized by the Chinese Communists. The film ends with Captain Wilder (Wayne) sailing into Hong Kong and 'freedom', greeted by the repeated sounding of steam whistles and ship's sirens from every vessel in the harbor.

Trump may be trying to be 'one of the boys' and to represent 'white America', but is he an anomaly of no lasting importance? Gideon Rachmen (2017) suggests than he is more than a blip in history. On a tour of American establishment redoubts – Wall Street, Washington, and the Kennedy School of Government at Harvard – this *Financial Times* journalist encountered what he describes as 'a cautious optimism that the Trump phenomenon can be contained, without doing lasting damage to the US'. As one Manhattan 'media type' put it, with a mixture of relief and contempt, Rachmen informs us: 'Trump lacks the self-discipline to be a fascist dictator' (cited in Rachmen, 2017).

However, as Rachmen points out, there is 'the likelihood that the Trump campaign has identified and nurtured profound discontents and divisions within the US that will outlast Mr Trump himself, and harden into a durable, far-right political movement'. If this happens, Rachmen concludes, 'it will create a cadre of determined ideologues and political footsoldiers. At that point, the early haphazard days of the Trump presidency may give way to something more determined – and more dangerous' (Rachmen, 2017). As I argue in the next chapter of this book, this is already well under way with the ascendancy of the 'alt-right'.

All this begs the question that many commentators have asked, 'is Donald Trump himself a fascist?' In his inaugural speech, Trump repeated a campaign slogan, '[w]e will make America great again'. While Hitler did use this in respect of Germany, so did Ronald Reagan in his campaign, and, indeed Margaret Thatcher in hers. More reminiscent of Nazi Germany was Trump's proclamation: 'We share one heart, one home, and one glorious destiny', and recalling the Nazi-associated 'tomorrow belongs to me', he promised, 'we are transferring power from Washington, D.C. and giving it back to you, the American People . . . because this moment is your moment: it belongs to you' (thus also encapsulating the National Will, like Thompson's hypothetical American fascist dictator). To seriously address the issue of whether Trump is a fascist, however, it is necessary to consider some key features of fascism.

Fascism: some key features

Fascism has no founding thinker, from which to draw out its key features, though, of course, Mussolini and Hitler loom large. Soiologist Michael

Mann (but see also Polyani, 1944; Paxton, 2004; Bosworth, 2006) has arguably provided the most comprehensive analysis of fascism to date, based on its actual existence in six European countries: Italy, Germany, Austria, Hungary, Romania, and Spain in the post-World War 1 era.[3] Put concisely, 'fascism is the pursuit of a transcendent and cleansing nation-statism through paramilitarism' (Mann, 2004, 13). Mann identifies five key terms connected with fascism: nationalism; statism; transcendence; cleansing; and paramilitarism (13–17). I will consider each in turn.

First, with respect to nationalism, 'fascists had a deep and populist commitment to an "organic" or "integral" nation', with an 'unusually strong sense of its "enemies",' both in other countries and at home. Fascists had 'a very low tolerance of ethnic or cultural diversity, since this would subvert the organic, integral unity of the nation'. Aggression against 'enemies' supposedly threatening this organic unity is the source of fascism's extremism. 'Race' is an ascribed characteristic, something we are born with and keep until we die. Fascists have a vision of the rebirth of an ancient nation, adapted to modern times (Mann, 2004, 13). To this I would add that fascism is against internationalism in all its forms, and, once in power, fascists attempt to centralize authority under a dictatorship and to promote belligerent nationalism, with only one party allowed and all others crushed.

Second, as far as statism is concerned, fascists worshipped state power, which 'needed to be authoritarian, embodying a singular, cohesive will expressed by a party elite adhering to the "leadership principle"' (Mann, 2004, 14). Fascist regimes exhibited a dialectic between 'movement' and 'bureaucracy', between 'permanent revolution' and 'totalitarianism' (Mann, 1997).[4] There was a tendency 'toward a singular, bureaucratic state [being] undercut by party and paramilitary activism and by deals with rival elites'. (Mann, 2004, 14).

Third, with respect to transcendence, rejecting both conservative notions that existing social order is harmonious and Marxist beliefs that harmony could be obtained only by overthrowing capitalism, fascist nation-statism held that social conflict could be 'transcended', first by repressing those who fomented strife by 'knocking both their heads together' and second by incorporating classes and other interest groups into 'state corporatist institutions' (Mann, 2004, 14). Citing Weber (1976, 503), Mann (2004, 14) stresses that fascists came from the political right, center, and left alike and drew support from all classes. Fascists attacked both capital (not per se but only particular types of profit-taking, usually by finance, or foreign or Jewish capitalists) and labor as well as attacking liberal democratic institutions (Mann, 2004, 14–15). I would stress here the fact that workers and their organizations are smashed through state terror and censorship. A response to the crisis of capitalism,[5] fascists believed they offered a revolutionary and supposedly achievable solution (Mann, 2004, 15), but, unlike Marxism, fascism lacked a general critique of capitalism, and in practice most fascist regimes leaned toward the established order and toward capitalism, though they involved the supposed creation of a 'new man' (Mann, 2004, 15).

Fourth, because opponents were seen as 'enemies', they were to be removed, and the nation 'cleansed' of them. 'Ethnic cleansing more often escalates, since the "enemy" is not permitted to assimilate' and most fascisms involved both ethnic and political cleansing (Mann, 2004, 16). To this, I would add that the most obvious example of 'cleansing' is, of course, the Holocaust, the key feature of which was the annihilation of millions of Jews, along with others perceived to be 'enemies' of the fascist state, or not worthy to be part of it. Virulent antisemitism, along with other extreme forms of racism, continues to be a key feature of fascism today, but the responses to the conditions that led to fascism between the two world wars will not be replicated exactly, and the scapegoats change to others not considered 'white' or 'Aryan'. Finally I would want to add here that fascists believe in 'racial breeding' for 'blood purity' (eugenics).

Mann's last key term is paramilitarism, both a key value and the key organizational form of fascism. It welled up spontaneously from below, but it was also elitist, 'supposedly representing the vanguard of the nation', violence being the key to the 'radicalism' of fascism (Mann, 2004, 16). As Mann (2004, 16) puts it succinctly:

Fascism was always uniformed, marching, armed, dangerous, and radically destabilizing of the existing order. What essentially distinguishes fascists from the many military and monarchical dictatorships of the world is this 'bottom-up' and violent quality of its paramilitarism.

I would add to Mann's five points that fascism is historically male supremacist and misogynistic, tending to celebrate a 'cult of masculinity' and the worship of and unbroken rule of a 'führer' or superior man – a demagogue leading a superior 'race' and gender. Fascism entails rampant sexism, whereby women's traditional and patriarchal roles are reinforced and made more rigid. Divorce and abortion are suppressed and the state takes full control of women and their bodies. Fascism tends to be homophobic (although there are some prominent contemporary gay neo-fascists), disablist, and, with respect to neo-fascism today, transphobic.

Historian Dave Renton (1999, 4) favors the Marxist theory of fascism most famously developed by Leon Trotsky, one that advances a dialectical theory of fascism, viewing it both as a reactionary ideology and a mass movement, where the ideology and the movement interact (3). We must not view fascism as simply a set of ideas, observable in the discussion of intellectuals, since ideas alone are not how fascism has been experienced either in the 1930s or today. As Renton (1999, 72–73) explains, fascism, according to Trotsky, was a product of contradictory circumstances, of the tension between the crisis of the elites and the failure of the socialist parties. The fascist movement thrived on a discrepancy between the mass base of its support and the reactionary nature of its goals. The social base of fascism was itself in antagonism, the petty bourgeoisie (small-scale capitalists such as shop-keepers and workers who manage the production, distribution and/or exchange of commodities and/or services owned by their bourgeois or capitalist employers) asserted its anger against capital by crushing the single class that could defeat capitalism (the working class). These contradictions were represented dialectically, in the sense that they were described as unstable. At the level of politics there would be a synthesis, a solution, either the working class would crush fascism or fascism would crush the working class. Trotsky derived a tactic to defeat fascism: the United Front, the notion of united action to defend working-class strongholds.

What distinguished Trotsky's use of the tactic was his insistence on the relationship between the offensive and the defensive. The immediate priority was united self-defense in the face of the fascist threat. However, in this process, the socialist militants should take control of their own workplaces (Renton, 1999, 73). Thus the process of anti-fascist defense becomes a process of anti-fascist offense: 'the smashing of fascism . . . would mean the direct introduction of the social revolution' (Trotsky, p. 232).

Renton's core argument is that fascism 'should be understood historically, through an examination of the relationship between its professed ideas and its actual practice, which involves looking at what it *did* at least as much as what it *said*' (Renton, 1999, 4).

Following from this, my aims in this book are to use the lens of public pedagogy in two ways. First I aim to try to understand what both Trump and those that surround him are doing and saying, and how this works to perpetuate hate and fascism (chapters 1–4) and second to demonstrate how public pedagogy is used to build resistance against fascism and for socialism (chapters 5 and 6).

Renton's position is that it is pointless to 'waste time, choosing *in precise detail* which ideas are fascist, and which not' (my emphasis) since different fascist movements 'have claimed to support radically different ideas' (Renton, 101). The analyses of Trump in this chapter and of the alt-right in the next should therefore be seen as attempts to ascertain what is specific about the state of fascism in the era of Trump towards the end of the second decade of the twenty-first century in the United States of America.

Is Trump a (neo-)fascist?

So, with a consideration of Mann's five key terms (slightly expanded) and Renton's observations of fascism in mind, I return to my earlier question, is President Donald J. Trump a (neo-)fascist? What about the fact that he reportedly owned a copy of Adolf Hitler's speeches and kept them in his bedside cabinet (Kentish, 2017b)? There is also his 'bullying tone, his scowl, and his jutting jaw' that recall Italian Fascist leader Benito Mussolini's 'absurd theatrics' (Paxton, 2017). However, despite his 'dramatic arrivals by plane (a public relations tactic pioneered by Adolf Hitler) and his excited dialogues with crowds chanting simple slogans ("U.S.A.! U.S.A.!" "Lock her up!")' (Paxton, 2017), Donald Trump is not Hitler or Mussolini. Fascism does not *define* Trump's (first) presidency, although a number of its features resonate with Trump.

First, with respect to nationalism, he has a deep and populist commitment to an integral nation and an 'unusually strong sense of its enemies' both at home and abroad, including 'aggression against them', and a very low tolerance of ethnic or cultural diversity – seen as a threat to the integral unity of the nation. I also suspect that he believes that 'race' is an ascribed characteristic. While Trump's belligerence overseas is well-documented, he shows no signs of banning other political parties at home, although it should be stressed that, in May 2018, he 'joked' about having a longer stint in office than is allotted by the Constitution: '[u]nless they give me an extension for the presidency, which I don't think the fake news media would be too happy about' (cited in Reese, 2018). As Ashely Reese (2018) points out, 'Trump really loves this joke! During [an earlier meeting with donors], Trump commented that China's president Xi Jingping has been given the title "president for life"'. Trump added, 'I think it's great. Maybe we'll want to give that a shot someday' (cited in Reese, 2018).

There are no visible signs of actual totalitarianism at the moment, if nothing else because of the constraints of the US federal system, and of course the strength of the popular movements against Trump and against fascism (including Antifa) (see chapter 5 of this book), combined with the general disapproval of and, indeed, disgust with Trump among large swathes of the American people.

Second, as far as statism is concerned, Trump is obsessed with power, is authoritarian, and insists on being a supreme leader who expresses a singular cohesive will to which all must conform (you agree with him and you're ok; disagree and you are the enemy, as exemplified, for example, by his excessive tweets – see chapter 2, pp. 37–42 for a discussion of Trump and Twitter).

Third, with respect to transcendence, Trump suppresses those who, in his eyes, foment strife by sacking them, and is engaged in trying to incorporate disgruntled workers into his version of state corporatism (tax cuts for rich *and* the workers – the former benefiting the latter; for the reality, see chapter 5 of this book, pp. 83–85). While Trump is not smashing workers and their organizations through state terror, he is seriously undermining trade union rights (see chapter 5, pp. 85–87).

Mann's fourth key term is 'cleansing'. While, as we shall see in this book, Trump is Islamophobic and racist, there is no 'racial breeding' or eugenics. Trump is certainly very keen to keep out or expel Muslims and people of color, as we shall see in chapter 2 of this book, but his public pedagogy and actions, extreme as they are, do not match the neo-Nazi-style actual 'ethnic cleansing' that we will see is inherent in the alt-right's concept of a white ethno-state (discussed in chapters 2, 3 and 4).

Trump is demagogic, revels in a cult of masculinity, and is transphobic (his attempt to ban transgender individuals serving in any capacity in the military is under challenge at the time of writing – see Chalfant, 2018). In addition, as Rachel Shabi (2017) notes:

> Trump's . . . attacks on a free press, overt lying, purging of the State Department's senior staff, firing of the acting attorney general, undermining of a democratic election process by claiming voter fraud, and attacks on the US judiciary – all evoke fascist hallmarks.

There is also, of course, Trump's slowness to condemn white nationalists and neo-Nazis, and his subsequent remarks and attitude, after the 'Unite the Right' rally in Charlottesville, Virginia, opposing the removal of a statue of Robert E. Lee (commander of the Army of Northern Virginia in the American Civil War) which ended in the death on August 12, 2017, of anti-fascist protestor Heather Heyer and injuries to some 35 others (Staff, 2017).[6] My fear is that this rally may be viewed as a historical turning point in the development of fascism in the US. Speaking in the lobby of Trump Tower three days after the killing, a combative Trump defended this slowness. Not generally known for his ability to reflect on issues before making a judgment. Trump behaves instinctively, and often tweets impulsively), on this occasion Trump repeated about a dozen times that he didn't want to make a quick statement without knowing the facts (Vox, 2017). At the same time, he compared the tearing down of Confederate monuments to the hypothetical removal of monuments to the so-called 'Founding Fathers', and said that counter-protesters deserve an equal amount of blame for the violence. He had previously said there were some 'very fine' people on both sides and that he blamed 'many sides', and later explicitly condemned right-wing racist elements. But in his Trump Tower press conference, he returned to the view that 'there are two sides to a story'. Trump also refused to call the murder of Heyer 'terrorism', dodged a question as to whether he 'missed a critical opportunity to help bring the country together', and, showing sympathy for those protesters who opposed the removal of the statue, Trump offered no such sympathy for the anti-fascists (Henderson, 2017). He said this of the anti-fascist protestors:

> What about the alt left[7] that came charging at, as you say, the alt right? Do they have any assemblage of guilt? What about the fact that they came charging with clubs in their hands swinging clubs? Do they have any problem?

> (cited in Nelson and Swanson, 2017)

Terry McAuliffe, Governor of Virginia, responded: 'Neo-Nazis, Klansmen and white supremacists came to Charlottesville heavily armed, spewing hatred and looking for a fight . . . This was not "both sides"' (cited in Henderson, 2017).

David Duke, a former 'grand wizard' of the Ku Klux Klan who was at the rally, knew which side Trump was really on when he tweeted, 'Thank you President Trump for your honesty and courage to tell the truth about Charlottesville and condemn the leftist terrorists' (cited in Henderson, 2017). UK *Guardian* columnist Richard Wolffe (2017) has no doubt where Trump's political allegiances lie:

> Donald J Trump quite literally sympathizes with fascists. He shares their worldview as easily as he shares their language and videos. He gives their voice and values the biggest platform in politics. He is a neo-fascist sympathizer in the mainstream of American politics, sitting at the heart of the West Wing and world power.

These quotes relate to Mann's fifth and final key feature of fascism – 'paramilitarism'. Trump is tolerant of armed fascists. In addition, he is, of course, totally pro-gun lobby and anti-gun control.

Fintan O'Toole (2018) argues that Trump is engaged in 'trial runs' for fascism by creating a universe of 'alternative facts' and by undermining moral boundaries, for example, alluding to Mexican children held in cages (see chapter 2, p. 33 of this book), 'let's see how my fans feel about crying babies in cages'. Following the dehumanisation of brown babies – so what if they are 'scarred for life?' – 'then the deeds can follow'.

Sexism

With respect to fascism and its rampant sexism and rigidly reinforced patri-archal roles, Trump is, of course, well known for his misogyny. This includes insults, other demeaning remarks, and numerous sexist comments. Here the public pedagogy of Trump is diametrically opposed to the intent of the feminist scholarship that has been the norm in public pedagogy (feminist public pedagogy scholars have focused on how public pedagogy has perpetuated sexism, as well as how it can subvert it) (Sandlin et al., 2011, 343–344). When once asked by Fox News reporter Megyn Kelly about referring to women as 'fat pigs, dogs, slobs and disgusting animals', Trump replied that he did not have time for 'political correctness',[8] and later went after Kelly on rival network CNN: 'You could see there was blood coming out of her eyes. Blood coming out of her wherever' (cited in Helmore and Jacobs, 2015).

In February 2018, Trump leaped to the defense of close White House aide Rob Porter who was forced to resign after two ex-wives accused him of domestic abuse, followed by the publication of photos that showed one of the women with a black eye. Failing to show any sympathy or concern for the women, Trump enthused, 'We wish him well, he worked very hard. We found out about it recently and I was surprised by it, but we certainly wish him well and it's a tough time for him' (cited in Smith, 2018a). Trump went on:

> He did a very good job when he was in the White House. And we hope he has a wonderful career and he will have a great career ahead of him. But it was very sad when we heard about it and certainly he's also very sad now.
>
> (cited in Smith, 2018a)

Trump concluded:

> He also, as you probably know, says he's innocent and I think you have to remember that. He said very strongly yesterday that he's innocent so you have to talk to him about that, but we absolutely wish him well, he did a very good job when he was at the White House.
>
> (cited in Smith, 2018a)

The editor of *Telegraph Women*, Claire Cohen (2017), has been tracking Trump's sexism and misogyny since the 1980s. For example, Trump once suggested that women should be 'punished' for having abortions[9]; made offensive 'jokes' and other remarks about his daughter; praised the physique of the French 'First Lady'; and made numerous attempts at flirting; as well as the infamous aforementioned boast of sexual assault, dismissed as 'locker room talk' (Cohen, 2017).[10] While his nomination of Brett Kavanagh to the Supreme Court is most ominous for the future of abortion rights, Trump is not able to reinforce a rigid patriarchy or take control of women and their bodies at the level of the state in the way that a fully totalitarian fascist regime could.

18   'One glorious destiny'

Disablism

As far as policies for people with disabilities are concerned, in both 2017 and 2018 the Trump administration called for cuts to a program that delivers meals to senior citizens and disabled people (Lartey, 2017; Guardian Staff, 2018). *Guardian* reporter Jamiles Lartey (2017), who volunteered with the program, states that this is a 'disaster' for the country's most vulnerable.

Moreover, as disability attorney, disability activist, and disabled person Katie Tastrom (2018) has pointed out, the Trump administration announced early in 2018 that it will allow states to require 'Medicaid recipients to participate in a work program or other form of approved "community engagement" in order to retain their health benefits'. Tastrom (2018) notes that, while there will supposedly be exceptions for disabled people, this new policy will be devastating in a number of ways. With respect to eligibility, no matter how broad states define 'disability', there will be disabled people who do not qualify for the exemption even though they should. Getting exempted from the work requirement owing to disability, she points out, will almost certainly require some kind of doctor's note or documentation. But if you do not have insurance, going to the right doctor (or any doctor at all) can be difficult, and those people will not be able to get the exemption needed (Tastrom, 2018). This will be compounded if one has an 'invisible' disability that cannot be easily and quickly diagnosed, and people whose income makes them eligible for Medicaid will not be able to afford upfront costs. Tastrom (2018) concludes:

> this is yet another attempt by the Trump administration to eliminate the modest gains in health insurance coverage made by the Affordable Care Act. The addition of a work requirement moves us further away from the idea of health care as a right and towards an America that does not provide a safety net for the most vulnerable, including people with disabilities.

This is indicative of at least an indifference on the part of Trump to the plight of disabled people, or, if we bear in mind an incident late in 2015, more likely contempt. During an election rally, Trump mocked *New York Times* reporter Serge Kovaleski, who has an impairment that visibly affects the flexibility and movement of his arms, arthrogryposis: 'You've got to see this guy', Trump said, before jerking his arms in an attempt to mock Kovaleski (cited in Borchers, 2017). Trump's response was that, when he singled out Kovaleski for ridicule, he did not intend to call attention to his impairment. His claim was that he was not aware of the impairment and 'was calling into question a reporter who had gotten nervous because he had changed his story' (cited in Borchers, 2017). In reality, as Callum Borchers

(2017) reveals, Trump was undoubtedly aware of Kovaleski's disability, since the latter had covered Trump long before he entered politics. As stated by Kovaleski himself, 'Donald and I were on a first-name basis for years' (cited in Borchers, 2017).

In Nazi Germany, physically and mentally disabled people were viewed as 'useless' to society, a threat to Aryan genetic purity, and therefore unworthy of life. At the beginning of World War II, disabled people were targeted for murder in what the Nazis referred to as the 'euthanasia' program (United States Holocaust Memorial Museum, 2018a). Euthanasia, literally 'good death', usually refers to the inducement of painless death for chronically or terminally ill people to prevent further suffering. In the Nazi context, however, it was a euphemism for a clandestine murder program (United States Holocaust Memorial Museum, 2018b), with about 200,000 disabled people murdered between 1940 and 1945 (United States Holocaust Memorial Museum, 2018a). This included children, and in August 1939, the Reich Ministry of the Interior circulated a decree 'requiring all physicians, nurses, and midwives to report newborn infants and children under the age of three who showed signs of severe mental or physical disability'. Following the decree, public health authorities began encouraging parents of children with disabilities to admit their children to a number of designated 'pediatric clinics', in reality, 'children's killing wards'. The age range was later extended to young people up to seventeen (United States Holocaust Memorial Museum, 2018b).

The 'euthanasia' or T-4 program became the model for the mass murder of Jews, Romas, and others in the concentration camps (United States Holocaust Memorial Museum, 2018a). These others included political prisoners (communists, socialists, and trade unionists); criminals; homosexuals; and Jehovah's Witnesses. Though not targeted for systematic murder like the Jewish and Roma peoples and the disabled, these 'others' often died in the camps from starvation, disease, exhaustion, and the sheer brutality of their treatment (United States Holocaust Memorial Museum, 2018c).

It would, of course, be ludicrous to suggest that Trump has any such plans, but, given the fact that he is supported by a groups of neo-Nazis and Hitler admirers in the alt-right (see chapters 3 and 4 of this book for a discussion), disdain for disabled people in the toxic fascistic and fascist mix that characterizes America today means that any form of disablism must surely ring warning bells. If Trump's pronouncements and actions with respect to disabled people do not amount to a public pedagogy for fascism (see chapters 3 and 4 of this book), they most certainly contribute to such a public pedagogy. Actor Meryl Streep's comment on the incident pertaining to Trump and Kovaleski was as follows:

> it was effective, and it did its job. It made its intended audience laugh and show their teeth. It was that moment when the person asking to sit

in the most respected seat in our country imitated a disabled reporter, someone he outranked in privilege, power, and the capacity to fight back. It kind of broke my heart, and I saw it, and I still can't get it out of my head because it wasn't in a movie. It was real life. And this instinct to humiliate when it's modeled by someone in the public platform by someone powerful, it filters down into everybody's life because it kind of gives permission for other people to do the same thing.

(cited in Borchers, 2017)

On balance, my own view is that, while Trump cannot be considered *a* fascist, he is 'fascistic', in the sense of leaning towards fascism, being open to fascist ideas, defending fascists on the ground, and ready perhaps to discuss fascism in private, or adopt one or more of fascist principles in public given the right set of political and economic circumstances. As such, he is perhaps fascism's most powerful elected ally in the second decade of twenty-first century America. 'Fascistic' allows for a necessary degree of fluidity. Trump is not able to be openly fascist or neo-fascist *at this particular conjuncture*. As Badiou (2016) puts it:

> what is the future of Trump? In some sense, we don't know, really, and maybe Trump doesn't know his proper destiny . . . In any case, we have really a symbol of the decomposition of the classical political oligarchy, and the birth of the new figure of a new fascism, with a future that we don't know.

The point is that fascism is a constant feature of capitalist societies, there to raise its profile when the political and economic climate permits. Trump's fluidity, therefore, may be thought of as convenient as the present conjecture. As American socialist theorist and activist, George Lavan Weissman warned:

> The military ruin of German and Italian fascism in WWII convinced most people that fascism had been destroyed for good and was so utterly discredited that it could never again entice any followers. Events since then, particularly the emergence of new fascist groups and tendencies in almost every capitalist country have dispelled such wishful thinking. The illusion that WWII was fought to make the world safe from fascism has gone the way of the earlier illusion that WWI was fought to make the world safe for democracy. The germ of fascism is endemic in capitalism; a crisis can raise it to epidemic proportions.

Weissman was writing in 1969. His warning remains equally if not more urgent half a century later, and takes on a heightened exigency in the Trump era. Weissman (1969) stresses the need for drastic countermeasures to be applied, specifically to build the revolutionary party. I will return to a consideration of resistance to Trump and fascism (chapter 5); and a revolutionary alternative – a public pedagogy against capitalism and for socialism (chapter 6).

Trump and climate change in late capitalism: fascism's pincer

A consensus on the potentially disastrous issue of climate change began to form in the 1980s (e.g. Hansen et al., 1981; Lorius Claude et al., 1985). As we hurtle towards the third decade of the twenty-first century, especially with the real possibility that Donald Trump will still be at the helm, climate change must be a top priority in any political program, and particularly one against capitalism and fascism and for socialism. I will return to this in chapter 6 of this book. At this stage, it is important to identify where we are at now. Friends of the Earth (2017) have summarized Trump's policies on climate change and other environmental issues. Trump has said the US will pull out of the Paris International Climate agreement of 2016 (the agreement responded to the global climate change threat by setting out a global temperature rise well below 2 degrees Celsius above pre-industrial levels and approved the pursuance of efforts to limit the temperature increase even further to 1.5 degrees Celsius); has taken steps to cut back the US Environmental Protection Agency; and is on record that global warming is a hoax invented by the Chinese to attack US manufacturing (Friends of the Earth, 2017).Trump's closest energy advisors all have very strong links to either the fossil fuel industry or climate-change denial groups, while long-term climate-change denier Rick Perry is Energy Secretary, and the CEO of ExxonMobil, Rex Tillerson, was Secretary of State. Trump's policy is to use American fossil fuel energy to the full (America possesses more combined coal, oil, and natural gas resources than any other nation on Earth), which, according to Friends of the Earth (2017) is 'an express ticket to deadly rises in global temperature'.

Interviewed by his longstanding 'friend' Piers Morgan, who asked whether he accepts the scientific consensus behind human-caused climate change, Trump replied, 'There is a cooling, and there's a heating' (cited in Mann, 2018). As Michael E. Mann (2018) points out, this is a version of the standard denialist trope that 'climate is always changing', whereas in reality, if one looks beyond year-to-year fluctuations caused by natural phenomena, such as El Niño, it becomes clear that our planet is steadily warming at a rate 'remarkably consistent' with module simulations produced by NASA (Mann, 2018). Mann notes that, the 'last four years were the warmest, globally, on record – and that record warmth cannot be explained in terms of natural climate variability', but is due to 'human-caused planetary warming'. In the same interview, Trump said, 'The ice caps were going to melt, they were going to be gone by now, but now they're setting records'. As Mann (2018) explains, in referring to the 'ice caps', Trump fails to distinguish between 'sea ice' that floats on water and that does not contribute to sea level rise when it melts and 'the continental ice sheets' in Greenland and Antarctic that store vast amounts of ice and are difficult to stop once they begin to melt. Trump, he goes on, is wrong on both counts, since by either definition of 'ice cap', records are being set for ice *loss*.

Mann (2018) continues, given that Donald Trump really appears to care only about himself, perhaps what he *really* means is that climate change is not a problem for *Donald Trump*. Even here, he is misguided. Mann refers to an article he co-authored (Garner et al., 2017) in which it was demonstrated that projected increases in sea level rise, along with more intense hurricanes, combine for a greatly increased risk of flood, indicating that mid-town Manhattan, including Trump Tower itself, is eventually within the danger zone, as is his golf course in Ireland, for which he hypocritically got special permission to build a wall, and his 'winter White House', Mar-a-Lago, in Florida (Mann, 2018). Mann concludes:

> When it comes to climate change policy in the current administration, our best hope is perhaps that Trump comes to realize that climate change is a threat not just to human civilization but to the one thing he cares about – Trump.
>
> (Mann, 2018)

Carl Beijer (2017; see also the first section of chapter 2 of this book) has argued that in late capitalism that features outsourcing, vast inequality, wage stagnation, and grim prospects for average Americans, we have arrived at fascism's pincer. By this he means that, on the one side we have looming ecological catastrophe and economic pathology – 'a discredited ruling ideology, declining standards of living, the memory of lived prosperity and absolute despair for the future', coupled with immigrants scapegoated by a wealthy elite 'controlling the most powerful propaganda apparatus in history'. On the other, there is ethnonationalism, the alt-right, and fascism (see chapters 3 and 4 of this book).

Conclusion

In this chapter, I assessed the relationship between Donald J. Trump and fascist ideology. I concluded that, although Trump bears a number of similarities with traditional fascism, it is too early to make a definitive judgment, and that he may more accurately at present be described as fascistic rather than fascist. In the course of my discussion, I considered not just the far-right and Trump's relation to it, but also the issues of sexism and disability. I concluded with a discussion of 'fascism's pincer', a real and tangible threat to our planet on multiple fronts. In the next chapter, I further explore Trump's racist/fascistic discourse as a public pedagogy of hate before moving on, in chapters 3 and 4, to an examination of the neo-fascist alt-right.

Notes

1 Following a dangerous remark from Kim Jong Un that 'a nuclear button is always on my desk', Trump tweeted in a puerile, elementary schoolboy-like and even more dangerous way: 'North Korean Leader Kim Jong Un just stated that the "Nuclear Button is on his desk at all times". Will someone from his depleted and food starved regime please inform him that I too have a Nuclear Button, but it is a much bigger & more powerful one than his, and my Button works' (Sky News, 2018). An explanation for this extraordinary behavior is provided by Michael Wolff, author of *Fire and Fury: Inside the Trump White House* (Wolff, 2018a). Interviewed on NBC in January 2018, Wolff stated that the one description that everyone gave about Trump is that he is 'like a child' (Wolff, 2018b). I return to a discussion of Wolff's book later in this chapter.
2 That such talk occurs in 'locker rooms' has subsequently been denied by those in the know (see, for example, Mindock, 2017).
3 For fascism's antecedents, see, for example, the many works of Ernst Jünger, Arthur Moeller van den Bruck, and Oswald Spengler.
4 Dialectic thinking, derived from George Wilhelm Friedrich Hegel, consists of (1) a beginning proposition – a thesis; (2) a negation of that thesis – the antithesis; and (3) a synthesis, whereby the two conflicting ideas are reconciled out of struggle to form a new proposition As well as having general explanatory power, the dialectic is at the core of Marxist theory. For Marxists, out of slave struggle came feudalism; feudalism begot capitalism; and out of class struggle, socialism becomes possible after capitalism's overthrow. Dialectical analysis, as we see here, and as will be developed shortly, can also explain other historical processes such as the growth of fascism and the possibilities of its overthrow.
5 I return to the concept of crisis, specifically from a Marxist perspective, in chapter 3 of this book and in chapter 6, where I discuss a public pedagogy for socialism, and whether socialism is possible in the US and elsewhere.
6 The Charlottesville rally in August 2017 has become the most infamous, but there were others in Pikeville and Shelbyville, Kentucky, in April and October respectively (Sunshine, 2017). Fifty alt-right supporters, including Richard Spencer, referred to extensively in this book, returned to Charlottesville in October 2017 (Burley, 2018).
7 Alt left or alt-left is a term created by white nationalists that no specific group self-identifies under (Vice News, 2017).
8 'Political correctness' or 'PC' is a pernicious concept invented by the Radical Right, which, unfortunately, has become common currency. The term was coined to imply that there exist (Left) political demagogues who seek to impose

their views on equality issues, in particular appropriate terminology, on the majority. In reality, nomenclature changes over time. Using current and acceptable nomenclature is about fostering a caring and inclusive society, not about 'political correctness'.

9 Trump spoke on January 19, 2018, the day before the end of his first year as president, to the forty-fifth pro-life anti-abortion rally, describing it as 'a movement born out of love'.

10 We shall see in chapters 3 and 4 how the alt-right's views on women follow closely those documented by the earlier fascist movements.

2 The wall, the travel ban, 'Pocahontas', 'sons of bitches' from 'shithole countries', and DACA

Trump's racist/fascistic discourse as a public pedagogy of hate

Introduction

Having dealt more generally with Trump's relationship with fascism in chapter 1 of this book, in this chapter I flesh this out with respect to his racist election campaign, his subsequent speeches, his slogans, his general policy agenda, and the way in which they and his tweets serve to promote a racist/fascistic public pedagogy of hate and to give legitimacy to fascism. Specifically, all this, in practice, amounts to encouraging his supporters and potential supporters to blame American's problems on Mexicans and Muslims and anti-fascists, and, as addressed in this chapter, to militate against what he sees as a 'liberal agenda'; to patronize and offend Native Americans and direct racist insults at African Americans and Haitians to instill fear, loathing, and derision prior to, in tandem with, or after the various elements of his racist and fascistic policy agenda. His use of 'fake news', to discredit anything that he feels undermines him, may be thought of as a kind of 'public pedagogy' in reverse, as far as certain news outlets are concerned: 'don't take any notice of them because you are being misinformed'.

The speeches and the agenda

The wall

'When Mexico sends its people, they're not sending their best . . . They're sending people that have lots of problems, and they're bringing those problems with us. They're bringing drugs. They're bringing crime. They're rapists' (Phillips, 2017). These are some of the words in Donald Trump's launch of his election campaign in 2015. And, although he added, 'And some, I assume, are good people' (Phillips, 2017), he was clearly intending to stir up hatred towards Mexican immigrants, and to justify his infamous pledge to build a wall along the Mexican border. Later in the same speech, Trump promised:

> I would build a great wall, and nobody builds walls better than me, believe me, and I'll build them very inexpensively, I will build a great, great wall on our southern border. And I will have Mexico pay for that wall.
>
> (cited in Phillips, 2017)

In December 2017, it was revealed that each of eight construction companies had produced 30ft high slab prototypes on display in the California scrubland of Trump's proposed 'big, beautiful' border wall (Milam, 2017). Sandlin et al. (2011, 350) refer to the 'ideological nature of display', as a form of public pedagogy, and while they are referring to historical sites such as museums, this also applies to *current* display. Thus Customs and Border Protection (CBP) states that the existence of these constructions sends a psychological message: 'The attention that these prototypes have brought to a worldwide audience has given us the ability to send the message' (CBP division chief Mario Villarreal, cited in Milam, 2017). 'The message', he went on, 'that we're a wonderful country, the greatest country in the world, and to those who want to come to the United States we highly recommend that they choose legal methods' (cited in Milam, 2017).

The actual reality caused by borders was articulated in public pedagogy by Brian Houston, who used the three minutes allowed for a brief reunification via an officially opened gate between the borders in San Diego's Friendship Park, to get married: 'We were very fortunate to be reunited and show that love has no borders. I wish the fence wasn't there. I think it is really sad, it is dividing families, dividing people, I don't understand the reasons for it' (cited in Milam, 2017). Enrique Morones, who runs 'Border Angels' that advocates human rights and humane immigration reform, has an explanation, clearly viewing the prototype walls as constituting a public pedagogy of hate rather than one of hope to come to a 'wonderful country': 'Without a doubt, it is a wall of hate . . . There isn't the money for it, it is just for show' (cited in Milam, 2017).

Following up Trump's anti-immigration speeches, in early January, 2018 the US Department of Homeland Security announced that it was terminating Temporary Protected Status (TPS) for more than a quarter of a million immigrants from El Salvador. The immigrants, a large majority of them poorer workers, were given 18 months, until September, 2019, to leave the US or be arrested and deported (Martin, 2018a). As Patrick Martin (2018a) argues, this decision signals the Trump administration's determination to put an end to the program entirely.

Also early in January 2018, International Youth and Students for Social Equality, reported 'an army of police, border guards, and immigration agents . . . descending on cities and towns across the country' with the US government 'separating parents from their children, spouses from each other, and workers from their jobsites' forcing them back to countries where, they remind us, 'poverty and violence are the by-products of decades of corporate exploitation and US-led imperialist war' (International Youth and Students for Social Equality, 2018). They state that the Trump administration is 'expanding a network of immigration detention camps to prepare for mass arrests and deportations on an unprecedented scale' (International Youth and Students for Social Equality, 2018).

At about the same time, the Trump administration rolled out the most right-wing immigration reform proposal since the Johnson-Reed Act of 1924 established immigration quotas to 'stabilize the ethnic composition' of the United States, one that will 'fundamentally alter the sociodemographic composition of the United States' (London, 2018a). If enacted as law, Eric London (2018a) estimates that the proposal will cut documented immigration by 22 million people over the next fifty years. According to the White House, the plan involves $25 billion to expand the wall along the US-Mexico border and to further militarize both borderlands and all air and sea ports (London, 2018a). The most dramatic cut to immigration, London goes on, will be the ending of the family-based petition system, whereby US citizens or legal permanent residents can 'petition their parents, unmarried adult children, married adult children, or siblings'. Legal permanent residents will also no longer be able to petition their spouses and minor children (London, 2018a). The Trump administration calls these restrictions 'protecting the nuclear family by emphasizing close familial relationships' (London, 2018a).

As a result, Eric London (2018a) explains, 'thousands of people who face persecution in their home towns and who have legal claims to refugee status will be denied the right to which they are entitled under international law'. London (2018a) concludes, meanwhile the hazardous nature of attempting to cross the border means that: 'the death toll in the desert continues to grow as thousands of immigrants seek shelter and family unification in the United States'.

In late March 2018, the US Department of Commerce announced that the 2020 Census will include a question for respondents asking whether or not they are US citizens (Meenakshi, 2018a). As Jagadeesan Meenakshi (2018a) explains, this serves the anti-immigrant witch-hunt in two ways:

> just posing the question will intimidate millions of immigrant families, whatever their own immigration status, if they have undocumented family members; and to the extent that any immigrants do respond, the

information will be used as a blueprint for future enforcement actions, highlighting the neighborhoods and communities to be targeted for raids by the Immigration and Customs Enforcement.

Islamophobia

During the election campaign, Trump delivered what might be his most infamous Islamophobic campaign pledge (Lind, 2015). Having first issued a press release, he read from his own speech in an attempt to blame *all* Muslims for Islamist terror: 'Donald J. Trump is calling for a total and complete shutdown of Muslims entering the United States until our country's representatives can figure out what the hell is going on'(cited in Krieg, 2017). As Gregory Krieg explains, the proposed ban cited dubious poll data from the Center for Social Policy, a fringe think tank founded and run by Frank Gaffney Jr., an anti-Islamic conspiracy theorist. One of Trump's first acts as president was the signing of an executive order in an attempt to implement a 'travel ban' targeting certain Muslim-majority nations. It was not until late in 2017 that The US Supreme Court ruled that the ban could be imposed while multiple court cases challenging it are resolved.

Also in his election campaign, Donald Trump built on his Islamophobic public pedagogy of hate by belittling the parents of a slain American Muslim soldier, Humayun Khan. The soldier's father, Khizr Khan, had strongly denounced Mr. Trump during the Democratic National Convention in a speech that was effectively the Democratic response to Trump's Islamophobia and proposed Muslim ban. Trump said that the soldier's father had delivered the entire speech because his mother was not 'allowed' to speak, the implication being that the soldier's mother was a subservient Muslim woman (Haberman and Oppel, 2016), thus using his public pedagogy to promote a sexist and racist stereotype. The soldier's father, Khizr Khan, lashed out at Trump, saying his wife had not spoken at the convention because it was too painful for her to talk about her son's death. Mr. Trump, he said, 'is devoid of feeling the pain of a mother who has sacrificed her son'. (cited in Haberman and Oppel, 2016). Later Ghazala Khan, the soldier's mother, said that when she saw her son's photograph on the screen behind her on the stage at the convention, 'I couldn't take it. I controlled myself at that time. It is very hard' (cited in Haberman and Oppel, 2016).

Indigenous Americans

Trump's racist/fascistic public pedagogy of hate unsurprisingly extends to Native Americans. He succeeded in transforming a White House ceremony to honor Navajo veterans of World War II into an event that involved first being condescending to his guests by telling them they were 'very, very special people . . . [who] were here long before any of us were here' (cited in Hirschfeld Davis, 2017). Second, he used the occasion to connect (in a pre-planned way?) the second part of this sentence with a further derisory remark about Senator Elizabeth Warren: 'Although we have a representative in Congress who, they say, was here a long time ago. They call her Pocahontas' (Warren identified as having Native American roots when a professor at Harvard Law School several decades before, and Trump had first referred to her thus on the 2016 campaign trail). As Julie Hirschfeld Davis (2017) further points out, Trump:

> made the remarks while standing in front of a portrait of President Andrew Jackson – a favorite of Mr. Trump's – who served as the nation's seventh president and signed the Indian Removal Act of 1830, which resulted in the mass displacement and deaths of Native Americans often referred to as the Trail of Tears.

This fore-fronting of Jackson could be seen as an attempt to use art, not as usually used in public pedagogy, as subversive of the dominant order (Sandlin et al., 2011, 347–350, 357–358), but in pursuit of a public pedagogy of hate.

Russell Begaye, present for the ceremony and the president of the Navajo Nation, referred to Trump's mention of Pocahontas as 'derogatory' and 'disrespectful to Indian nations', while Warren noted: 'It should have been a celebration of their incredible service, but Donald Trump couldn't make it through without tossing in a racial slur' (cited in Hirschfeld Davis, 2017).

It is most unlikely that Trump could be alluding to the real historical personage, but rather the popular Disney animation. Thus the public pedagogy of hate here works at several levels. First, there is Trump's reference to a cartoon character. Giroux (1998, 256) has examined the Disney corporation in terms of a 'teaching machine', while elsewhere, he has provided an analysis of gender and racial stereotyping in Disney films (Giroux, 1999, 124, cited in Sandlin et al., 2011, 345). Some Native Americans have suggested that Trump is using the word Pocahontas in a way that evokes the term, 'squaw' to taunt the senator, a term that, at least in modern usage, has both sexist and racist connotations (Capriccioso, 2017).

Second, Giroux has also commented on how Disney's nostalgic 'pedagogy of innocence' (Giroux, 1999, 124) is enacted through strategies of 'escapism, historical forgetting, and repressive pedagogy' (p. 127) which strip public memory of its 'historical, social, and political context' (p. 127) (cited in Sandlin et al., 2011, 345–346). In a similar fashion, Ali Nahdee (2017) has described Disney's 'Pocahontas' as historically inaccurate (Disney consulted with historians, but did not draw on their analyses), offensive and harmful, noting excessive use of anti-Native terminology. She also castigates the company for referencing the genocide of Native Americans visually and in song, and for suggesting that love and empathy can stop the horrors of colonial violence. As a counter to Trump's remarks about her, while addressing the National Congress of American Indians in February 2018, Warren stated, 'For far too long, your story has been pushed aside, to be trotted out only in cartoons and commercials. Every time someone brings up my family's story, I'm going to use it to lift up the story of your families and your communities' (cited in Shugerman, 2018).

A different president might have used the White House ceremony to honor America's indigenous peoples in a non-patronizing way; and to commend them for the common struggle that they and other (more recent) US citizens waged against fascism during World War 11 (thus constituting a public pedagogy against fascism), perhaps in front of a portrait of a prominent Native American.

Trump's contempt for Native Americans was also revealed in one of his first acts as president. On January 24, 2017, Trump ordered the Army Corps to withdraw the notice of its intent to prepare an Environmental Impact Statement (EIS) and to issue the right to cross for the Dakota Access Pipeline (DAPL), under the Standing Rock Sioux Tribe's water supply (the right to cross had been denied by the Obama administration that had sought to explore alternative routes). As Ardalan Raghian, freelance journalist who was at Standing Rock for several months during the resistance to the pipeline, wrote in early 2018:

> A new year and five oil spills later, the flowing of oil through the . . . DAPL . . . continues to be a threat to tribal survival. As the Tribe battles to shut down the oil flow through the courts, new information detailing how the pipeline was wrongly placed through Lake Oahe – the Tribe's main source of drinking water – is emerging.
>
> (Raghian, 2018)

As Raghian explains the decision to move the DAPL from a route north of Bismarck (population, 90% white) to the traditional lands of the Sioux and under Lake Oahe, impacted the 84% Native population. The United States Army Corps of Engineers, he goes on, cooperated with the company, Dakota Access, LLC, to prepare an environmental justice analysis that deliberately excluded or obscured evidence of disproportionate 'racial' impact, in violation of Title VI of the Civil Rights Act of 1964.

'Sons of bitches' from 'shithole countries'

In September 2017, Trump launched an extraordinary attack on National Football League (NFL) players who were kneeling during the US national anthem as part of continuing protests against racism in the US. At a Republican rally, Trump ranted, 'Wouldn't you love to see one of these NFL owners, when somebody disrespects our flag, to say, "Get that son of a bitch off the field right now. Out! He's fired!" '(cited in Graham, 2017). Following that racist and sexist rant (racist because a large majority of NFL players are black – Goodman, 2017; sexist for his use of 'bitch', 'son of a bitch', being such a common expression in the US that its essential sexism can be overlooked, though possibly not for the misogynist Trump), he went on to urge spectators to leave the stadium when it happens (Graham, 2017). Surveys have shown that a majority of white Americans disapprove of the protests, while most African Americans support them (Guardian Sport, 2017). However, it is worth noting that a more recent CNN report (Sparks, 2018) points out that polling 'in the last year has been split half and half on support for players in the NFL kneeling during the National Anthem, and a lot of the variance depends on how the questions are asked in the surveys'. Nevertheless, Patrick Martin (2017) is right to argue that 'Trump sought to provoke as much outrage as possible, particularly among the black athletes . . . and in that way arouse his ultra-right and fascistic social base'. Martin (2017) argues that the most brazenly racist aspect of this affair was a tweet by Trump soon after, in which he hailed the performance of NASCAR (National Association for Stock Car Auto Racing), whose drivers who are nearly all white, stating that he was 'so proud' of the Association, after reports suggested that any individual who protested against the national anthem would be sacked (de Menezes, 2017). The public pedagogical intent, in my view, could not be clearer, the message being: 'These African Americans are unpatriotic "sons of bitches" and should be ostracized, while white stock car drivers are "fine Americans," of whom we should be proud'.

In January 2018, remarks by Trump describing immigrants from Africa and Haiti as coming from 'shithole countries' was condemned as racist by United Nations human rights spokesperson Rupert Colville: 'I'm sorry but there's no other word one can use but racist. You cannot dismiss entire countries and continents as "shitholes," whose entire populations, who are not white, are therefore not welcome' (Griffiths and Smith-Spark, 2018). Trump had suggested that the US should bring more immigrants from Norway.

Although Trump subsequently denied using those exact words, it follows on from previous comments that 15,000 Haitians who received US visas 'all have AIDS' and 40,000 Nigerians would never 'go back to their huts' after seeing the US, comments also denied by the White House (Mark, 2017a). The pedagogical implications are obvious. Cedric Richmond, Democratic Representative and chair of the Congressional Black Caucus, said Trump's comments were 'yet another confirmation of his racially insensitive and ignorant views' that reinforce 'the concerns that we hear every day, that the President's slogan Make America Great Again is really code for Make America White Again' (cited in The Associated Press, 2018).[1]

The day after the alleged 'shithole' remark, Trump signed a proclamation honoring Martin Luther King Jr.'s life and civil rights work. As he smiled and greeted those standing beside him, reporters erupted with questions about his statement on African and Haitian immigrants. 'Mr. President, are you a racist?' April Ryan of American Urban Radio Network asked. 'Mr. President, will you respond to these serious questions about your statement, sir?' Trump ignored all questions and exited the Roosevelt Room (Finley, 2018).

In South Africa, the African National Congress government labeled the remark as 'extremely offensive', with the country's media full of denunciations and ridicule of Trump. One news outlet, the *Daily Maverick*, clearly recalling the burning torches at the Charlottesville rally, wrote that an event at the White House 'is soon to include [Ku Klux Klan] hoods and tiki torches at this rate'. (cited in Cogan, 2018). Meanwhile, after an emergency session to discuss Mr Trump's remarks, a group of 54 African ambassadors to the United Nations said it was 'concerned at the continuing and growing trend from the US administration toward Africa and people of African descent to denigrate the continent and people of colour'. The group noted that it was 'extremely appalled at, and strongly condemns the outrageous, racist, and xenophobic remarks by the president of the United States of America as widely reported by the media' and demanded a 'retraction and an apology' (cited in Chung and Culbertson, 2018).

Criminalization of immigrants

The following month (February 2018), the anti-immigrant rhetoric and policy initiative continued apace. In a speech to the Conservative Political Action Conference (CPAC) that Jagadeesan Meenakshi (2018b) describes as rambling and 'quite extraordinary in its ignorance, bigotry and distortion of reality', Trump presented a world in which the United States was 'under attack by swarms of criminals, rapists, hit-and-run drivers, human traffickers, all of whom are "aliens" who have been let into the country "because our immigration laws are so bad"' (Meenakshi, 2018b). 'In a particularly vile and repellant [to which I would add racist and sexist] manner', Meenakshi goes on, Trump compared immigrants to a vicious, poisonous snake that kills a foolish yet 'tender woman' who provides it shelter. Trump claimed that the country was over-run by 'animals . . . who cut [people] into little pieces' and who, according to Trump, were protected by laws that favored them, and provided them with safe harbor (Meenakshi, 2018b): 'laws are just against us . . . we are letting people in, and its going to be a lot of trouble' (cited in Meenakshi, 2018b). He promised that his administration was up to the task of 'protecting like never before' (cited in Meenakshi, 2018b). 'In 2017', Trump concluded, 'our brave ICE officers arrested more than 100,000 criminal aliens who have committed tens of thousands of crimes' (cited in Meenakshi, 2018b). Trump pledged that he was 'going to take care of the country. Okay? We're going to take care of the country' (cited in Meenakshi, 2018b).

The consequences of Trump's fascistic viewpoints reached a crescendo some four months later when photographs, video, and recordings of young children in metal cages, with just tin foil blankets for comfort, in a US detention center crying for their mothers and fathers were shown around the world. This prompted a huge amount of condemnation from the public, the media, politicians, and others, and forced Trump to sign an executive order on June 20, 2018, to keep migrant families together. However, there was no indication of what would happen to families already separated, for which there is apparently no organized database. Prior to this, Trump had for weeks refused to reverse a 'zero tolerance' enforcement policy, which led to the separation of 2,300 children from their families (Gambino and Laughland, 2018) in an attempt to put pressure on Congress for a $25 billion border wall, having realized that his earlier 'promise' to make Mexico pay was not viable.

On June 24, 2018, on CNN News, having visited a Texas detention center, Democrat Representative Barbara Lee described having witnessed a three-year-old boy and a three-year-old girl on their own in cells sleeping on cement floors. She was not allowed to take in a camera or a cell phone. Lee described the cages as prisons and also referred to mothers in another cell who did not know where their children were.

Her remarks were made just before it was revealed by Time magazine that a draft memo that it had obtained indicated a growing military responsibility that had resulted from Trump's 'zero tolerance' policy (Elliott and Hennigan, 2018). According to the document, the US Navy is preparing plans to construct sprawling detention centers, in the form of 'temporary and austere' tent cities for tens of thousands of immigrants on remote bases in California, Alabama, and Arizona. In addition, as Philip Elliott and W. J. Hennigan (2018) explain, what 'began as a crackdown on immigrants crossing the border illegally has now spread to the departments of Justice, Homeland Security, Defense and Health and Human Services'. The document makes reference to adding 10,000 additional individuals each month to the centers (Elliott and Hennigan, 2018).

Around the same time, Trump tweeted for speedy deportations that bypass any judicial process: 'When somebody comes in, we must immediately, with no Judges or Court Cases, bring them back from where they came' (cited in BBC News, 2018).

2018 State of the Union Address and DACA

I will end this section of the chapter with a discussion of the immigration plan announced in Trump's 2018 State of the Union address and with a brief look at what immigration policies look like on the ground. The address, given just before his speech to the CPAC, has been praised mainly because it was mediocre, uninspiring, and *not terrible* (Harriot, 2018), and because Trump managed to stick to the script. However, a closer reading reveals that the Trump racist agenda remained fully on course. Trump announced an immigration plan with four pillars.

While the second, third, and fourth obviously have racist intents, dealing with building a wall on the Southern border and 'hiring more heroes . . . to keep our communities safe'; ending 'randomly [handing] out green cards without any regard for skill, merit, or the safety of our people', and 'moving towards a merit-based immigration system' (cited in CNN Politics, 2018) (which translates into 'only admitting white people'; Harriot, 2018); and protecting 'the nuclear family by ending chain migration . . . [and] virtually unlimited numbers of distant relatives', and 'limiting sponsorships to spouses' (cited in CNN Politics, 2018), the first might at first appear more liberal. As Trump detailed it:

> The first pillar of our framework generously offers a path to citizenship for 1.8 million illegal immigrants who were brought here by their parents at a young age – that covers almost three times more people than the previous administration. Under our plan, those who meet education and work requirements, and show good moral character, will be able to become full citizens of the United States.
>
> (cited in CNN Politics, 2018)

The background to this is that in September 2017, it had been announced that DACA (Deferred Action for Childhood Arrivals), the program that gives temporary protection to undocumented migrants who arrived in the US as children, affecting 800,000 people, would end. As Joanna Walters (2017a) explains, DACA is a federal government program in 2012 under Barack Obama to permit people brought to the US 'illegally' as children the temporary right to live, study, and work in America. If they pass vetting, action to deport them is deferred for two years, with a chance to renew, and they become eligible for basics like a driving license, college enrollment or a work permit. Those protected under DACA, mainly from Mexico, El Salvador, Guatemala, and Honduras and aged 15 to 36, are known as 'Dreamers' since DACA was a compromise devised by the Obama administration after its failure to pass the Development, Relief, and Education for Alien

Minors (Dream) Act, which would have offered those who had arrived illegally as children the chance of permanent legal residency. The ripping up of DACA was part of Trump's election pledge to make the deportation of the US's estimated 11 million-plus undocumented persons a top priority (Walters, 2017a).

As Professor of Public Interest Law and Chicana/o Studies at the University of California, Davis, Kevin Johnson (2018) points out, the March 2018 deadline for ending the DACA program, in early March 2018 is on hold on account of a federal court ruling. Since its inception, DACA has helped nearly 800,000 young undocumented immigrants, whereas just over 1.8 million actually met the DACA criteria. The reason only 800,000 received it is because they 'had to be in or have graduated from high school, had to have obtained a general education development certificate, or had to have served in the military' (Johnson, 2018). In addition, anyone with a criminal record of a felony or more than two misdemeanors or who posed 'a threat to national security or public safety' was prohibited from receiving DACA (Johnson, 2018). Finally, some who were eligible did not apply for fear that signing up might lead to them or their families being deported. As Johnson (2018) points out, after Trump assumed office a number of DACA recipients were arrested and detained. While it appears to maintain the same requirements that existed for DACA, Trump's proposal of a path to citizenship for 1.8 million, would limit relief to about only one-half of Dreamers, ignoring the 1.8 million that never registered for DACA (Johnson, 2018). Johnson summarizes the reality of Trump's first pillar of his immigration plan: it would cover only about 16 percent of the total undocumented population of over 11 million; it would leave about 9 million undocumented immigrants subject to deportation; millions of undocumented immigrants who have lived and worked in the US for years would not be eligible for legalization and face possible deportation, affecting people with families (including US citizen children).

Trump's reign of terror

Eric London (2018b) describes what he refers to as 'Trump's reign of terror' on the streets of California:

> On a sunny Sunday morning in Napa County, California this past weekend, the 14-year-old daughter of a construction worker named Armando Nunez Salgado filmed through tears as her father was dragged away by Immigrations and Customs Enforcement (ICE) who parked outside their home in unmarked cars, walked into the family's backyard through a side gate, and arrested him. One ICE agent is heard

telling Nunez's daughter, Isabel, 'If you turn the camera off, we'll tell you where we're going to take him'.

As London (2018b) points out, ICE conducted ten other arrests that day across Northern California, although their main purpose was to make their dangerous presence known, congregating in front of movie theaters, taco stands, and other public spaces. 'These sightings', he goes on, 'caused false rumors of raids to spread across the region, prompting panic'. The arrests took place after an unprecedented public warning by the mayor of Oakland that ICE 'is preparing to conduct an operation in the Bay Area, including Oakland, starting as soon as within the next 24 hours' (cited in London, 2018b), an announcement that itself came in the wake of Trump's warning that California would 'see crime like nobody has ever seen crime in this country' unless immigrants are deported (cited in London, 2018b).

As London (2018b) explains, the Trump administration is targeting California 'in a thuggish act of political retribution', because the state passed a 'sanctuary state' bill in 2017 that prohibits state agencies from handing immigrants' information over to federal immigration officials without a court order. In ICE Director Thomas Homan's words, California is 'about to see a lot more special agents, a lot more deportation officers'. This warning was followed by raids on about 100 7-Eleven convenience stores located across the country, including many in California, the aim being to intimidate immigrant workers who comprise a large portion of the stores' clientele. As Erik Schnabel, Development and Communications Manager for San Jose-based Services Immigrant Rights & Education Network (SIREN) said, 'It's really clear that California is being targeted. It is pretty clear that fear and intimidation is what the Trump administration intended' (cited in London, 2018b). London (2018b) concludes:

> The federal government's intimidation campaign is aimed at undercutting the state's economy, which is heavily dependent on the super exploitation of immigrant labor. The efforts to spread fear and panic are also aimed at transforming the immigrant population into a permanent, deeply impoverished underclass living on the fringes of society. Immigrants in fear of deportation raids are less likely to bring their children to school, seek medical help for health problems or emergencies, seek public aid, report crimes to police, or even leave their homes for work or errands.

In April, 2018, using fascistic language, Trump claimed 'our country is being stolen' and that a caravan 'had better be stopped', thus denying asylum applications from nearly 200 immigrants, escaping violence, war, and poverty in Honduras, El Salvador, and Guatemala, and acting in flagrant violation of international law (London, 2018c). Eric London explains the background to the situation: 'US imperialism has transformed these countries into social disaster zones'.

He goes on to point out that in El Salvador the US government trained and armed the military dictatorships that massacred tens of thousands of peasants and workers, and in Guatemala 'ethnically cleansed' villages of similar numbers of indigenous Mayans in the 1980s (London, 2018c). In Honduras, the US backed and funded 'contra' forces that carried out death squad terror.

It would seem that just as 'Make America Great Again' is really code for 'Make America White Again', so the wall; the Islamophobia; the contempt for Native Americans; for 'sons of bitches' from 'shithole countries', together with the criminalization and deportation of immigrants, the caging of their children and accompanying 'reign of terror all amount to vast public pedagogies of hate and related racist policy initiatives, and serve to embolden Trump's neo-Nazi base (see chapters 3 and 4).

The Trump persona and Twitter: simplicity, impulsivity, and incivility

In January 2018, Trump canceled a trip to open a new US embassy in London, stating on Twitter:

> Reason I canceled my trip to London is that I am not a big fan of the Obama Administration having sold perhaps the best located and finest embassy in London for 'peanuts', only to build a new one in an off location for 1.2 billion dollars. Bad deal.
>
> (cited in Helsel and Smith, 2018)

It is likely that the real reason Trump canceled the visit was concern about mass anti-Trump demonstrations in the UK. With respect to his stated reason, this forms part of a series of condemnations he has made of Barack Obama.[2] In addition to the billionaire capitalist Trump's view on a bad business deal, perhaps another reason might be that, in Trump's twisted mind, Obama is no more than a 'shithole person' from a 'shithole continent'.

Trump's use of Twitter brings his political public pedagogy directly to the public. His abundance of verbal abuse via Twitter is, of course, also his major way of communicating his insults to the world. Brian L. Ott (2017, 60), though he does not refer to the concept of 'public pedagogy', explains succinctly the way in which Twitter acts as a perfect medium for a public pedagogy of hate:

> every communication medium trains our consciousness in particular ways [and] Twitter ultimately trains us to devalue others, thereby, cultivating mean and malicious discourse

As a mode of communication, Ott (2017, 60) goes on, Twitter is defined by three key features simplicity, impulsivity, and incivility. As Matt Kapko (2016) puts it, by demanding simplicity, Twitter undermines our capacity to discuss and subsequently to think about issues and events in more complex ways (cited in Ott, 2017, 61). With respect to impulsivity, because of wireless technology, we can tweet from virtually anywhere at any time, and, tweeting requires little effort, forethought, reflection or consideration of consequences. Finally, since it depersonalizes interactions, Twitter creates a context in which people do not consider how their interaction may affect others (Tait, 2016, cited in Ott, 2017, 62). Given that 'negative sentiment' is the key to popularity on Twitter (Thelwall et al., 2011, 415, cited in Ott, 2017, 62), and since simplicity, impulsivity, and incivility define Trump's personality, Twitter is an ideal platform for him. As Ott (2017, 62) concludes, 'All of this means that Twitter breeds dark, degrading, and dehumanizing discourse; it breeds vitriol and violence; in short it breeds Donald Trump'.[3]

Insights into Trump's personality are revealed in a book by Michael Wolff (Wolff, 2018a). As Hannah Thomas-Peter (2018a) explains, the American journalist and author had 'unchecked access to Trump World for weeks on end, chatting on and off the record with anyone he fancied'. There are allegations that Trump did not want to win the election; that he lacks knowledge and is unable to absorb basic information and that he is regarded as stupid (Thomas-Peter, 2018a). Patrick Martin (2018b) comments:

> What can be gleaned from the excerpts published so far is a portrait of a man who is profoundly, willfully ignorant about anything that does not touch directly on his own ability to make money and his own personal comfort: in other words, a figure quite representative of the worst traits of the American corporate elite.

Michael Wolff (2018b) stated in an interview that the unanimous description of Trump was that he was 'like a child' (see chapter 1, endnote 1 of this book). In the same interview, Wolff explained that what this meant was that he has 'a need for immediate gratification', 'it's all about him'.

Drawing further on Wolff's (2018a) book, Martin notes that Trump spends his entire day on the phone with a narrow circle of cronies and watches cable television, interrupted by occasional meetings with his staff and cabinet, during most of which Trump talks and does not listen. Martin quotes a particularly telling passage:

> Here, arguably, was the central issue of the Trump presidency, informing every aspect of Trumpian policy and leadership: He didn't process information in any conventional sense. He didn't read. He didn't really

even skim. Some believed that for all practical purposes he was no more than semi-literate. He trusted his own expertise – no matter how paltry or irrelevant – more than anyone else's. He was often confident, but he was just as often paralyzed, less a savant than a figure of sputtering and dangerous insecurities, whose instinctive response was to lash out and behave as if his gut, however confused, was in fact in some clear and forceful way telling him what to do.

(Wolff, 2018a, cited in Martin, 2018b)

In August 2017, according to the Pew Research Center, two-thirds (67%) of Americans reported that they get at least some of their news on social media (Shearer and Gottfried, 2017). While Ott (2017, 65) recognizes that mainstream news is also part of the problem, he concludes (writing at a time when the percentage was 62%) with the particular threat posed by social media:

This is alarming, *profoundly so*, since the 'news' content on social media regularly features fake and misleading stories from sources devoid of editorial standards. Moreover, it is specifically targeted to users based on their political proclivities

Ott is referring to fake news.[4] Citing Olivia Solon (2016), Ott (2017, 65) concludes that the result is the creation of ideological silos, powerful echo chambers of misinformation that, owing to confirmation bias, reaffirm our existing beliefs. Given his millions of followers, and given that his half a dozen tweets are reported almost daily (sometimes several times a day) on mainstream news outlets, Trump's public pedagogy of hate is well-known, although to his supporters it is seen as a rational response to the world as he and they see it. It needs to be stressed in the context of this book, however, that Trump's tweets go beyond racism, in the sense that they are also fascistic and play into the hands of the alt-right's vision of a white ethno-state. I return to alt-right's conception of a white ethno-state in chapters 2, 3, and 4 of this book.

The public pedagogy of hate in Trump's tweets is also aimed directly at white people in general who feel let down by the 'American Dream' of upward mobility, and also abandoned by the traditional establishment. As Chip Berlet (2015) puts it:

Trump's rhetorical propaganda is aimed at appealing to a growing base of angry and frustrated White middle and working class people. In a script broadcast by Trump *ad nauseum*, he is telling them who to blame for their slipping economic, political, and social status.

According to research by Rory McVeigh, people who join far-right move-ments tend to be convinced they are losing or about to lose status, power, or privilege in one or more of three civic arenas: economic, political, or social (McVeigh, 1999, 2009)

By 'mobilizing resentment' (Hardisty, 1999, cited in Berlet, 2015):

> Trump . . . capture[s] their hearts and minds by telling them their anger is justified and then point[s] them at scapegoats rather than the insti-tutions that have failed them. A culture permeated by the legacies of White supremacy[5] leads the White middle and working class to blame their real downward mobility on people of color and 'non-White' immigrants, and in that way reproduces both structural racism and the class-based power of the one percent.

Trump is intent on the normalization, acceptance, and promotion of fascism, as in his response to Charlottesville discussed earlier in this chapter. Here Trump was using public pedagogy at a press conference both to appease the fascist demonstrators and to try to 'educate' the public that some alt-right supporters are 'very fine people' (Krieg, 2017), and that, while some anti-fascists are 'fine people' too, there is blame on both sides. Even his initial silence about the events may be seen as a form of public pedagogy. Not saying anything could have been perceived by some as acknowledging that nothing too untoward happened.

Another blatant attempt to normalize and promote fascism was a retweet of a quote attributed to Mussolini and his response to his retweet in a TV interview. Trump retweeted from a parody account, @ilduce2016, that has a profile picture that is a composite of Mr. Trump's hair and Mussolini's face (Haberman, 2016). Here is the quote from @ilduce2016: 'It is better to live one day as a lion than 100 years as a sheep' – '@realDonaldTrump #MakeAmericaGreatAgain' 11:13 AM - Feb 28, 2016 (cited in Haberman, 2016).

In the subsequent interview on NBC, Trump said he was unaware that it had been a quote from Mussolini. But, as Maggie Haberman (2016) points out, he didn't seem to care: 'It's a very good quote. I didn't know who said it, but what difference does it make if it was Mussolini or somebody else – it's a very good quote' (cited in Haberman, 2016). When asked if he wanted to be associated with Mussolini, Trump replied flippantly, 'No, I want to be associated with interesting quotes. Hey, it got your attention, didn't it?' (cited in Haberman, 2016).

On yet another occasion, Trump decided to give a platform to British fas-cist group 'Britain First'. Late in 2017, Trump retweeted to his 43.6 million followers three anti-Muslim videos, originally tweeted by Jayda Fransen,

Britain First's deputy leader. Fransen is disposed to carrying a large wooden cross and organizes 'Christian patrols' and 'Mosque invasions' in areas with large Muslim populations.

Fransen was delighted with the attention and unexpected boost to global fascism and tweeted in upper case:

THE PRESIDENT OF THE UNITED STATES, DONALD TRUMP, HAS RETWEETED THREE OF DEPUTY LEADER JAYDA FRAN-SEN'S TWITTER VIDEOS! DONALD TRUMP HIMSELF HAS RETWEETED THESE VIDEOS AND HAS AROUND 44 MILLION FOLLOWERS! GOD BLESS YOU TRUMP! GOD BLESS AMER-ICA! OCS[6]

@JaydaBF@realDonaldTrump 12:05 PM - Nov 29, 2017

In the US, David Duke, obviously equally impressed, wrote on Twitter, 'Thank God for Trump! That's why we love him!' (cited in Mazelis, 2017), while in a direct appeal for help from Trump for the cause, Fransen stated, 'Thanks for the retweets @realDonaldTrump I'm facing prison for criticising Islam. Britain is now Sharia compliant, I need your help!' (cited in Weaver et al., 2017). As Matthew Weaver et al. (2017) point out, on this occasion, Trump did not retweet on the spur of the moment or without due consideration:

The Islamophobic videos were originally tweeted by Fransen on Tuesday afternoon and Wednesday morning before being picked up by Trump. They were not sequentially posted, meaning the president would have had to scroll through her timeline before picking out which videos to retweet.

When asked in 2015 if he considered retweets endorsements, Trump replied, 'You know, I retweet, I retweet for a reason'. (Klein and Schleifer, 2015).[7] Apart from the obvious intention of promoting Islamophobia, and other forms of racism, to millions worldwide (Dearden, 2017), Trump also uses public pedagogy via Twitter to normalize and legitimize fascism. Such tweets go beyond the incivility that characterizes that website. As Giroux (2018) remarks in relation to Trump's 'shithole' remark, but equally applicable to Trump's public pedagogy in general:

His remarks . . . smack of an appeal to the sordid discourse of racial purity. There is much more at work here than a politics of incivility. Behind Trump's use of vulgarity and his disparagement of countries that are poor and non-white lies the terrifying discourse of white supremacy, ethnic cleansing and the politics of disposability. This is a vocabulary that considers some individuals and groups not only face-less and voiceless, but excess, redundant and subject to expulsion. The endpoint of the language of disposability is a form of social death, or even worse.[8]

Conclusion

In the first part of this chapter, I discussed how Trump's racist/fascistic dis-course acted as a public pedagogy of hate, with reference to his speeches and his agenda, first with respect to 'the wall', then to Islamophobia and to Indigenous Americans, before considering his remarks about African Amer-icans and the continent of Africa. I concluded the first part of the chapter with an analysis of Trump's response to DACA (Deferred Action for Child-hood Arrivals) and to immigration more generally. In the second part of the chapter, I addressed the issue of the Trump persona and its relationship with Twitter. Twitter, I concluded, with its emphasis on simplicity, impulsivity, and incivility is an ideal vehicle for the president and his public pedagogy of hate.

Trump's lack of theoretical sophistication about politics in general means that his rhetoric differs from the alt-right in the sense that the aims of the lat-ter are more complex. They involve, in Renton's terms, both the creation of a mass movement and a reactionary ideology that is erudite and *academic*. The alt-right's public pedagogy is a pubic pedagogy for fascism, whose central platform is the promotion of the imperative need for the building of a white ethno-state. If Trump's tweets represent the simple, impulsive, and uncivil arm of the far right in today's United States, then the alt-right is, in the main, its intellectual arm. It is to the alt-right that I now turn.

Notes

1 Trump holds similar views on the ethnic composition of Europe, commenting that immigration policies in that continent are changing its 'fabric', and destroying European culture and that accepting migrants from the middle east and Africa is 'a very negative thing', and further that European countries need to 'watch them-selves' because, '[y]ou are changing culture, you are changing a lot of things': 'I think allowing millions and millions of people to come into Europe is very, very sad', cited in Miller and Colvin (2018). In chapters 2 and 3, I discuss the alt-right notion of a white ethno-state.
2 For an analysis of Trump's largely one-sided attacks on Obama, including the months in 2010 when Trump stoked the flames of the 'false birther theory' that suggested that Obama was born outside the US, and therefore ineligible to serve as its president, see Liptak and Jones (2017).

3 In this chapter, I concentrate on Trump's use of Twitter to further his public pedagogy of hate. It needs to be pointed out that Trump also uses Twitter to boast of his 'achievements' and to praise his 'friends'. As Christian Fuchs (2017, 57) puts it:

> Twitter-politics is a politics of 140 character soundbites that consist of a world polarised into friends and enemies. Via Twitter, Trump broadcasts news about how his personal friend/enemy-scheme evolves. There are two sides: The side of the friends, whom he characterises as great, impressive, nice, successful, and talented.
> And the side of the enemies, whom he characterises as bad, biased, failing, inaccurate, dishonest, nasty, not nice, one-sided, overrated, poor, rude, sad, terrible, untalented, or wrong. Trump's politics is a world of polar opposites, in which representatives of the two sides have completely opposed characteristics.

While Twitter militates strongly towards impulsivity and incivility, Twitter, of course, does not *have* to be either. Also, while Twitter, because of word constraints, *has* to be simple, it can be clever and thought-provoking.

4 In what might qualify as the most compelling (unwitting) example of real 'fake news', as opposed to the way Trump uses the term – not to refer to information that is self-evidently false – but to any news that is critical of him or his prejudices, he tweeted:

> Actually, throughout my life, my two greatest assets have been mental stability and being, like, really smart. Crooked Hillary Clinton also played these cards very hard and, as everyone knows, went down in flames. I went from VERY successful businessman, to top T.V. Star. . .
> . . . to President of the United States (on my first try). I think that would qualify as not smart, but genius . . . and a very stable genius at that!

(Baynes, 2018)

5 It would seem that Berlet is using 'white supremacy' in its traditional sense here, rather than the way in which Critical Race Theorists use the term to refer to 'everyday racism'. For a Marxist critique of the Critical Race (CRT) usage of 'white supremacy', see Cole (2017a, 85–89); see also Cole (2017b, 301–308).
6 OCS stands for 'Onward Christian Soldiers' (Hartley-Parkinson, 2017).
7 For a compilation of everything Donald Trump has tweeted since he became president, see *Los Angeles Times* (ongoing); see also the Trump Twitter Archive (ongoing).
8 For a definitive list of Trump's racism, see Leonhardt and Prasad Philbrickjan (2018).

3 'Our glorious leader has ascended to God Emperor! Hail Trump! Hail our people! Hail victory!'

The alt-right and public pedagogies of hate and for fascism

Introduction

In this chapter, I begin with a brief consideration of the political and economic backdrop, thirty-five years of neoliberal capitalism in the US (of which the devastating 2008 global economic crisis formed a part) that helped create Trump the president, and gave a major boost to the far right, paving the way for the alt-right to move towards the mainstream. Neoliberal capitalism and its aggressive 'free market' and anti-worker diktats have resulted in a high degree of alienation among workers, especially since the crisis. The way it was handled spawned deep discontent and anger directed towards the established political elite, including the Clintons, resulting in what Henry Giroux (2017) refers to as '*Fascism, American-Style*'. In chapter 1, I considered Donald J. Trump's relationship with fascism, including his sexism and disablism. In chapter 2, I moved on to his racist and fascistic rhetoric and accompanying agenda targeted at people of color in the US and elsewhere, as well as his use of Twitter to promote a public pedagogy of hate and add legitimacy to fascism. I now direct my attention on the alt-right itself. I begin with its public pedagogy for fascism and its agenda, focusing on some key alt-right figures, including its founder, Richard Spencer. I examine a pivotal introductory guide to the alt-right by openly neo-Nazi Andrew Anglin that clearly demonstrates that the alt-right is a new (neo-) fascist movement, but with links to older fringe white supremacist movements, rather than just a component of right-wing conservatism. I conclude with a brief discussion of the public pedagogy for fascism of alt-right activist, Christopher Cantwell, conspicuous as part of the alt-right's armed wing and a central figure at Charlottesville. As with many other alt-right figures, his public pedagogical activities involve a combination of street activity and internet propaganda.

The ascendancy of Trump and the alt-right: political and economic backdrop

Neoliberal capitalism

The ascendancy of Trump and the accompanying attempts to mainstream the far right in US society need to be viewed in the context of the witnessing in large parts of the world of 'a dramatic weakening, if not a simple breakdown, of the authority of the established political classes and political parties' that Nancy Fraser (2017) refers to as 'a *global* political crisis'. This crisis is the direct result of the accumulated effects of the imposition nearly half a century ago of a form of capitalism that has brought unprecedented wealth to the few and parallel poverty and immiseration to the many. Neoliberal capitalism dates back to Augusto Pinochet in Chile in 1973, after a US-backed military coup ousted democratically elected socialist Salvador Allende (see Maisuria and Cole, 2017). Pinochet's brutal military junta and its harsh repressive measures, which included the banning of trade unions and making labor power as flexible as possible, inspired both Ronald Reagan in the US and Margaret Thatcher in the UK in the 1970s and 1980s (Reagan started his presidency in 1981 and Thatcher became leader of the Conservative Party in 1975 and Prime Minister in 1979). For example, Reagan, in his first year of office, fired more than 11,000 air traffic controllers who ignored his order to return to work (Glass, 2008), while one of Thatcher's biggest neoliberal victories was the smashing of the great miners' strike of 1984–1985.

Derived from the work of Frederick Hayek (1960) and others, neoliberalism sees competition as the defining characteristic of human relations, with the market ruling supreme – theorized as a more efficient system than anything that could be planned or designed. Whatever impedes the rule of the market such as state provision or regulation, progressive taxation or trade union activity needs to be swept away. It was argued that unrestricted 'entrepreneurs would create the wealth that would trickle down to everyone' (Monbiot, 2016). This stands in stark contrast to historical evidence (e.g. Lawson, 2016) and contemporary statistics (see the first section of chapter 5: 'Reality: Global and US capitalism 2018').

George Monbiot (2016) summarizes Hayek's (1960) main arguments: rejection of political freedom; of universal rights, of human equality and of the sharing of wealth; and with the ultra-rich leading society and free to do as they wish without being constrained by the public interest or public opinion. He sums up the results of Thatcherism and Reaganomics: massive tax cuts for the rich; the crushing of trade unions; reduction in public housing; deregulation; privatization; outsourcing; and competition in public services, all proposed by Hayek and his disciples, notably Milton Friedman, who was advisor to both Reagan and Thatcher. In the US, this neoliberal hegemony was maintained under both Bushes, Bill Clinton, and Barack Obama (for a discussion of the relationships between neoliberalism, global capitalism and public pedagogy, see Sandlin et al 2011. 352–354).

Upsurge in globalization and financialization

The liberalization of the capitalist economy entailed a major upsurge in globalization, of which a key component was financialization. Michael Peters and Petar Jandrić (2018, 53), cited in McLaren, 2018, have captured financialization's essence as follows:

> Financialization is a systematic transformation of capitalism based on the massive expansion of the financial sector, where finance companies have taken over from banks as major financial institutions and banks have moved away from old lending practices to operate directly in capital markets. Large previously non-financial multinational corporations have acquired new financial capacities to operate and gain leverage in financial markets. . . . In general, financialization represents the dominance of financial markets over declining production by the traditional industrial economy, and a corresponding abstraction of 'fictionalized' capital that increasingly controls price mechanisms but adds little or nothing to real value.

At the heart of the 2008 global economic crisis was nearly $5 trillion worth of basically worthless US mortgage loans. The Emergency Economic Stabilization Act of 2008, in effect the bailout of the banks, and signed into law by George W. Bush, authorized the US Secretary to the Treasury to spend up to $700 billion to purchase distressed assets, especially mortgage-backed securities and provide cash directly to the banks and other institutions. However, as Judy Beishon (2018) puts it, while the 'deep financial crisis . . . shook the capitalist elites to their core . . . [the] stimulus and bailout packages have been a bonanza for the wealthiest'. She goes on, instead of 'investment to advance society, the "captains of industry" have gorged themselves on obscene pay levels, stock options and dividends . . . partly financed by reducing the share of total wealth produced that goes to their workforces' (Beishon, 2018). At the same time, workers' conditions and wellbeing have been ground further downwards (Beishon, 2018) (see the first section of chapter 5 of this book for the reality of capitalism in 2018 with respect to inequality and poverty).

As Monbiot (2016) puts it, although popularly associated with Reagan, financialization was substantially implemented and consolidated by Bill Clinton. Notably, it was Bill Clinton who, in 1991, repealed the almost moribund

Glass-Steagall Act of 1933 (the law kept commercial banks separate from investment firms). Clinton also presided over 'the dismantling of barriers to, and protections from, the free movement of capital; the deregulation of banking and the ballooning of predatory debt; deindustrialization, the weakening of unions, and the spread of precarious, badly paid work' (Fraser, 2017).

Growing disillusionment

All these blatant attempts to skew the wealth of the world more and more in favor of the super-rich has led to deep skepticism, as has the ongoing relentless pursuit of US imperialism (e.g. Cole, 2017a, 141–150). As Graeme Wood (2017) argues:

> The world may be no more complicated now than it was in the past, but exposure to more aspects of it has proved disorienting to many Americans. Far-off wars and economies determine, or seem to determine, the fates of more and more people. Government has grown so complicated and abstract that people have come to doubt its abstractions altogether, and swap them for the comforting, visceral truths of power and identity.
>
> (Wood, 2017)

In summary, the global political crisis is the direct result of decades of unbridled neoliberal capitalism, of which masses of people had become estranged, and that had led to seething discontent, anger, rage, and frustration in large part directed at the established political elite. As Monbiot (2016) concludes, the 'man who sank Hillary Clinton's bid for the presidency was not Donald Trump. It was her husband'. While Hillary and the rest of her establishment politicians tried to hide their hardline neoliberal capitalist agenda 'under the banner of equality, justice and prosperity for all',[1] it was Donald Trump who seized the opportunity to pursue the vote of the dispossessed, by cynically claiming to come to the rescue of the poor white workers in the rust belts and elsewhere[2] who refused to vote for the establishment figure Hillary Clinton and provided a groundswell of support for her opponent who (falsely) promised to Make America Great Again and to create a decent future for the forgotten white working class. It was Trump's unexpected victory that also emboldened, energized, and served to bring a degree of legitimacy to the alt-right.

The alt-right: public pedagogy for fascism and agenda

If Trump, as is argued in chapter 1 of this book, is not currently identifiable as *a* fascist or *a* neo-fascist, many of his supporters manifestly are. The most prominent conglomeration of these supporters is known as the alt-right. Although it is supported by a range of far-right elements such as the Ku Klux Klan, white nationalists, neo-Confederates, and anti-government 'patriot' movements (Walters, 2017b), the alt-right is basically a 'new' movement spawned on the internet. I put 'new' in inverted commas and refer to a *movement* rather than new ideology because the alt-right in its current guise is essentially a throwback to traditional European twentieth-century fascism, specifically Nazism, but 'new' in terms of having arisen in the second decade of the twentieth century, and, therefore, differing from pre-internet forms of fascism in its propensity for promoting its ideas in a variety of web formats. As Anton Shekhovtsov, editor of the ibidem-Verlag book series 'Explorations of the Far Right', succinctly puts it, 'the "alt-right" is not a name for some new right-wing movement; it's a fancy hipster self-representation of neo-Nazis' (cited in Weiss, 2017).

The white ethno-state

Founded by the far right activist Richard Spencer in 2010, the alt-right's long-term goal is the establishment of a white ethno-state. There are similarities between Hitler's beliefs about 'non-Aryans', Mussolini's core 'philosophy' and alt-right's desire for such a state. As Mussolini put it in 1920:

> When dealing with such a race as Slavic – inferior and barbaric – we must not pursue the carrot, but the stick policy. We should not be afraid of new victims. The Italian border should run across the Brenner Pass, Monte Nevoso and the Dinaric Alps. I would say we can easily sacrifice 500,000 barbaric Slavs for 50,000 Italians.
>
> (cited in Verginella, 2011)

As Spencer sates it in a similar vein, presumably referring (primarily) to 'the stick policy' – the genocide of Native Americans:

> We conquered this continent. Whether it's nice to say that or not, we won. We got to define what America means. We got to define what this continent means. America, at the end of the day, belongs to white men.
>
> (cited in Hunter, 2017)[3]

It should be noted here how the use of 'belongs to white men' in connection with the white ethno-state resonates with the Nazi-associated 'tomorrow belongs to me', as does a part of Trump's inaugural discussed in chapter 1 of this book (see p. 10). In addition, 'white *men*' is consistent with what, as we shall shortly see, is the alt-right's fascist-consistent misogyny and anti-feminism.

In conversation with *The Atlantic* correspondent Graeme Wood, after referring to this concept of a new 'post-American' state, Spencer 'joked' that he would like to be the *'Kulturminister'* of such a state (Wood, 2017).[4] Spencer has given the examples of Poland and Israel as modern ethno-states (Ruptly, 2017).

Anglin (2016) spells out what else, in addition to 'striking the root and removing the Jews from our societies', the creation of new white ethno-states would involve for him:

> We believe in mass deportations of all non-White immigrants, regardless of whether or not they were born here. This would include, in America, a repatriation to Africa of the descendants of slaves (or an allocation of autonomous territory for them within our current borders).

More recently The Right Stuff, a neo-Nazi website that hosts 'The Daily Shoah' ('Shoah' is Hebrew for the Holocaust) ran a blog post arguing that the most appropriate thing to do would be to kill all black people in Africa, and use the continent for 'living space' (in German 'lebensraum'): following Hitler's rise to power, lebensraum was an ideological principle of Nazism that provided justification for territorial expansion into East-Central Europe (Bullock and Trombley, 1999, 473). As the blog post put it, 'Extermination of the brown hordes in their homelands could give vast new territories to us. They are ours for the taking' (cited in Burley, 2018). It went to argue that racial struggle is inevitable, and as is predicted by nature, the superior species often wipes out the inferior (Burley, 2018). As Shane Burley (2018) continues, a regular host on the 'The Daily Shoah' who goes by the pseudonym 'Jayoh' has referred to himself openly as an 'exterminationist', believing that nationalists would have to actively exterminate Black Africans, fearing they would eventually enter into white nations and corrupt them.

All these 'policy positions' on ethnic cleansing would, of course, need a totalitarian state to achieve their objectives, and therefore resonate with Mann's (2004, 13–14) 'statism' (anti-democracy) as well as his 'nationalism' (no ethnic and cultural diversity) and 'cleansing' features of fascism discussed in chapter 1 of this book (see pp. 11–12).

Modern-day colonialism

Burley (2018) argues that, while many alt-right supporters would not go so far as to advocate the annihilation of a continent of people, they are moving more towards the concept of modern-day colonialism. For example, 'Spencer's rhetoric has changed from the idea of isolated tribal states to envisioning the white [ethno-state] as a great empire', fulfilling what he sees as white people's 'Faustian spirit', the internal drive to explore and conquer

(Burley, 2018). Spencer's own 'Alt Right Politics' podcast, Burley points out, 'regularly celebrates European colonialism and expansionism, discussing colonialism as something that is a sum benefit for the colonized' and, in order not to become 'humiliated peoples', as Spencer views indigenous peoples, white Europeans, echoing Mann's (2004, 13–17) 'transcendence' and 'cleansing' features of fascism (see chapter 1, pp. 11–12 of this book), must win the 'racial conflict' (Burley, 2018). As Burley (2018) concludes, while the alt-right used to argue that rather than ruling others, they favored 'nationalism for all peoples', 'the idea that non-whites need to be controlled by whites is again gaining popularity, even if many of the thought leaders would deny this when pressed' (Burley, 2018).

For Spencer, however, 'race' is not just about color, as in the common US categories of black, white, Asian, Native American and Latinx (the last formulation to replace Latina/o is becoming increasingly commonplace; no doubt Spencer would say something different), but is more akin to 'volksgeist' (the spirit of a people), based on the work of Johann Gottfried von Herder. Andrew Hamilton (2011) defines 'volkgeist' as follows:

> In a holistic sense, race consists of dimensions beyond physical anthropology or population genetics. Just as every distinct population shares common morphological and physiological traits, despite within group variation they likewise express unique group psychology, intelligence, behavior, character, morals and, ultimately, culture and civilization.

The volksgeist Spencer associates with is white Christendom, including European peoples roughly from Iberia to the Caucasus (Wood, 2017).

The alt-right or the neo-Nazis?

All this raises the question of whether 'alt-right' is a meaningful description for the new movement. Shekhovtsov (2017), for one, insists that the events in Charlottesville demonstrated that the neo-Nazis have successfully appropriated the term, 'alt-right', a 'cover for whitewashing the entire spectrum of neo-Nazi beliefs', so it must be abandoned by the mainstream media and replaced by 'neo-Nazi'. This echoes a statement by former neo-Nazi Christian Picciolini, a key figure in the American skinhead movement in the 1980s before he rejected its racist ideology. He told CBC News:

> What Richard Spencer is doing today is what we did 28 years ago as very open neo-Nazis: The rhetoric is the same, the ideology is the same, the words are a little more massaged, more palatable.
>
> (cited in Hunter, 2017)

Not so for some of the neo-Nazis at the 'Unite the Right' rally, which had supporters displaying Nazi symbols and chanting the extremely unpalatable 'Jews will not replace us' and 'blood and soil'. The latter was a key slogan of Nazi ideology: ('blut und boden' in German), and meaning that ethnic identity is based on only blood descent and the territory in which an individual lives, thus celebrating rural farmers and peasants as virtuous members of the Aryan 'race' (Wagner, 2017).

Moreover, at the end of the gathering, both Duke and Spencer gave speeches, with the former stating, 'The truth is the American media, and the American political system, and the American Federal Reserve, is dominated by a tiny minority: the Jewish Zionist cause', and the latter mocking Charlottesville's Jewish mayor, Mike Signer: 'Little Mayor Signer – "See-ner" – how do you pronounce the little creep's name?'. His followers responded, 'Jew, Jew, Jew' (cited in Sunshine, 2017).

The 'Unite the Right' rally is *par excellence* an example of public pedagogy, combining the use of a 'public monument' (Carrier, 2006, cited in Sandlin et al., 2011, 350; Sandlin et al., 2011), or also 'public art space' to foster public debate about its meaning and the political possibilities it produces (Moisio and Suoranta, 2006, cited in Sandlin et al., 2011, 348), and indeed a historical site symbolizing 'white superiority' (Sandlin et al., 2011, 351), in this case the Robert E. Lee statue, which highlighted the 'ideological nature of display' (Sandlin et al., 2011, 350). The rally was also an opportunity for alt-right to use a public space to 'educate' the public about their antisemitism: 'Jews will not replace us' and 'blood and soil'.

As CNN reporter Eric Bradner (2016) explains, serving to certify Richard Spencer's neo-Nazi credentials, 'Hail Trump! Hail our people! Hail victory' is the accolade and rallying cry chosen by Spencer at an alt-right meeting when Trump was elected president ('Hail victory' in German is 'Sieg heil'). On hearing this 'call to arms', some members of the audience gave Nazi salutes. In his speech, Spencer referred to 'the black political machines' and 'Latino housekeepers' – as he attacked Hillary Clinton's minority supporters:

> Her coalition was made up of mutually hostile tribes only united out of a hatred of 'whitey' – that is to say, out of a hatred of us.
>
> (Spencer, cited in Bradner, 2016)

In the section of his speech dedicated to criticizing both the media and Jews, and referring to journalists who covered the presidential election, Spencer wondered if 'these people are people at all, or instead soulless golem' (in Jewish folklore an animated anthropomorphic being created entirely from clay or mud). He also used a Nazi-era propaganda term meaning 'lying press' to describe reporters, citing 'the mainstream media – or perhaps we should refer to them in the original German, lugenpresse' (cited in Bradner, 2016).

Spencer's views on being white also figured in this speech:

> To be white is to be a striver, a crusader, an explorer and a conqueror. We build, we produce, we go upward. . . . For us, it is conquer or die. This is a unique burden for the white man, that our fate is entirely in our hands. And it is appropriate because within us, within the very blood in our veins as children of the sun, lies the potential for greatness. That is the great struggle we are called to. We are not meant to live in shame and weakness and disgrace. We were not meant to beg for moral valida-tion from some of the most despicable creatures to ever populate the planet. We were meant to overcome – overcome all of it. Because that is natural and normal for us. Because for us, as Europeans, it is only normal again when we are great again.
>
> (cited in Wood, 2017)

Once again, 'white *man*' is consistent with alt-right sexism and misogyny. Spencer describes:

> the concepts that are now designated 'problematic' and associated with whiteness – power, strength, beauty, agency, accomplishment. Whites do and other groups don't . . . We don't exploit other groups. We don't gain anything from their presence. They need us, and not the other way around.
>
> (cited in Wood, 2017)

The blatant public pedagogy for fascism in this 'Hail Trump' speech, which contains for national correspondent for *The Atlantic* Graeme Wood (2017) 'among the most orthodox Nazi statements ever uttered by an American public figure', represents a counterinstitutional space in which the edu-cational activity of speech and performative display contrast with the established culture (Sandlin et al., 2011, 348), but not, of course, in the pro-gressive way Sandlin et al were thinking about. An online video of excerpts from the event produced by *The Atlantic* (2016) has, at the time of writing, had nearly 3 million hits, creating a reactionary public pedagogical event of significant proportions.

How the alt-right public pedagogy for fascism works

A central question posed by Sandlin et al. (2011, 359) is '*how* the various sites, spaces, products, and places identified as public pedagogy actually operate as *pedagogy*', how they work. Although he does not make use of the concept of 'public pedagogy', Wood (2017) shows how Spencer's public pedagogy works, comparing Spencer to William F. Buckley Jr., preeminent conservative in the late twentieth century after whom Spencer aspires. As Wood (2017) explains, 'Spencer has been casing out a role for himself as a human alarm clock in this process of awakening'. 'Buckley', Wood points out, 'had a flair for theater', injecting his ideas into the public consciousness both openly and insidiously, by announcing them loudly, and by making roguish and heretical asides in otherwise sleepy moments of debate'. 'The poison', he goes on, 'entered the bloodstream with only the slightest prick felt – but felt it was, and many a viewer came to love and hate Buckley for the thrill of intellectual disorientation'. 'Spencer . . . tries to work a lowbrow form of the same magic, through the obnoxious, needling harassment that he and his shitlords [true believers in the alt-right] call trolling'. In Spencer's own words: 'There is a value to shock. You can open someone's mind with something shocking. There is something to be said for not just retreating into a bourgeois, boring version of my ideas' (cited in Wood, 2017). Referring to the Nazi salutes at Spencer's 'Hail Trump' speech, Wood (2017) notes how they 'provoked sputtering rage from . . . [correct-thinking] people, and between sputters the enraged dropped their intellectual guard. It is hard to be enraged and analytical all at once, and many chose rage'. 'But', as Wood argues, 'rage confers no defense against ideas'. As Spencer informs Wood:

> Take the term *ethno-state*. I don't want to sound like I'm bragging, but *ethno-state* has now been used in mainstream sources! That term would never be used before. They're not necessarily original ideas to me, but they've never been brought to the mainstream in this way'.
>
> (cited in Wood, 2017)

Wood notes how 'Spencer wears a permanent naughty grin . . . the grin of a man who cannot believe his luck at being a fascist just at fascism's moment of American ascent'. 'His revolutionary movement', Wood concludes, 'is unlikely to succeed. But it is, I fear, authentic and durable'.

The 'extermination of whites': 'a Jewish conspiracy'

The *Daily Stormer* is a neo-Nazi news and commentary website aptly named after 'the gutter Nazi propaganda sheet known as *Der Stürmer*' (Southern Poverty Law Center, 2017) – and founded by Andrew Anglin in 2013 to replace his previous website, *Total Fascism*. As a result of being rejected by domain registers, it is sometimes offline or on the dark web. In a candid piece published in 2016, Anglin states that the 'core concept of [the alt-right], upon which all else is based, is that Whites are undergoing an extermination'. He then reveals the antisemitism that, as in Nazi Germany, is at the core of the alt-right movement. This 'extermination' occurs 'via mass immigration into White countries which was enabled by a corrosive liberal ideology of White self-hatred, and that the Jews are at the center of this agenda'. Antisemitism is, he points out, the 'defining value of the movement'. The 'foundation of its ideology', he explains, 'is that the Jews are fundamentally opposed to the White race and Western civilization and so must be confronted and ultimately removed from White societies completely':

> It is now fully-documented that Jews are behind mass-immigration, feminism, the news media and Hollywood, pornography, the global banking system, global communism, the homosexual political agenda, the wars in the Middle East and virtually everything else the Alt-Right is opposed to. This is, to a shocking extent, simply admitted by the Jews themselves.
>
> (Anglin, 2016)

Thus, for Anglin, in a very real sense, 'defeating and physically removing the Jews will solve every other problem' (Anglin, 2016).

The alt-right views the election of Trump as the beginning of the revolutionary transition to the white ethno-state. As Anglin exclaimed:

> Our Glorious Leader has ascended to God Emperor. Make no mistake about it: we did this. If it were not for us, it wouldn't have been possible . . . the White race is back in the game. And if we're playing, no one can beat us. The winning is not going to stop.
>
> (cited in Garcia, 2016)

Duke tweeted on Trump's election night:

> [t]his is one of the most exciting nights of my life. Make no mistake about it, our people have played a huge role in electing Trump! We have the moral high ground, 100%. Donald J Trump now has the chance to become one of the greatest Americans to have ever lived.
>
> (cited in England, 2016)

Recalling Renton's focus on a dialectical theory of fascism as a reactionary ideology *and* a mass movement (see chapter 1, pp. 12–13 of this book), but updated for the twenty-first century, Anglin (2016) articulates the uniqueness of the alt-right in the present conjuncture: 'The Alt-Right is a "mass movement" in the truest possible sense of the term, a type of mass-movement that could only exist on the internet . . . . [It is] an online mob of disenfranchised and mostly anonymous, mostly young White men'. He goes on to explain how the public pedagogy works:

> Some of the ways the movement presents itself can be confusing to the mainstream, given the level of irony involved. The amount of humor and vulgarity confuses people. The true nature of the movement, however, is serious and idealistic. We have in this new millennium an extremely nihilistic culture. From the point when I first became active in what has become the Alt-Right movement, it was my contention that in an age of nihilism, absolute idealism must be couched in irony in order to be taken seriously. This is because anyone who attempts to present himself as serious will immediately be viewed as the opposite through the jaded lens of our post-modern milieu.
>
> (Anglin, 2016)

A concise history of the neo-Nazi alt-right

Anglin then gives a brief history of the movement which eventually coalesced around a center-point at the time of Trump's election campaign. He identifies five important elements in this history of the alt-right.

First there is anonymous intellectual meme ('a concept or idea that spreads "virally" from one person to another via the internet', usually an image of a person or animal with a funny or witty caption [Beal, 2018]) and trolling culture that emerged in the 00s on a public discussion forum on 4chan's /pol/, which consists of an imageboard website (one that mostly posts images) to which users usually contribute anonymously. Richard Seymour (2016) has defined trolls as 'the self-styled pranksters of the internet, a subculture of wind-up merchants who will say anything they can to provoke unwary victims, then delight in the outrage that follows'. They do what they do for the 'lulz', a corruption of 'LOL', 'Laughing Out Loud'. In Whitney Phillips' (2016) words, 'lulz', the form of enjoyment they get from others' distress, can be viewed as schadenfreude with more bite (cited in Seymour, 2016). A key feature of 4chan's /pol/ was antisemitic and racist 'jokes' that 'became serious, as people realized they were based on fact' [sic], Anglin (2016) informs us. It became a haven for virulent antisemites and aggressive racists, he points out, and the 'tone of the Alt-Right is drawn directly from these roots on 4chan' (Anglin, 2016):

> On 4chan, the Jewish problem was analyzed by news junkies and history buffs, feminism was deconstructed by sexually frustrated young

men, and race was considered based on the actual data on the issue. The rehabilitation of Adolf Hitler and the NSDAP largely took place on 4chan.

(Anglin, 2016)

'This newly formulated Nazi ideology', Anglin points out, 'was then combined with the established troll culture, based on memes, hilarious images designed to transmit cultural concepts', together with 'lulz' (Anglin, 2016). This, according to Anglin, made promoting the right-wing agenda not only meaningful, but also extremely funny. 'The Alt-Right', Anglin concludes, carries with it that spirit of fun. A public pedagogy of hate and for fascism, based on propaganda, therefore, was and is promoted with 'humor'.[5] The type of 'troll storm' initiated by Anglin is exemplified by the following incident where his actual practice links up with his professed ideas (Renton, 1999, 4) (see chapter 1 of this book). It began after a dispute involving Sherry Spencer, Richard Spencer's mother, and another Whitefish, Montana, resident, Tanya Gersh. As Mallory Simon (2018) explains, Gersh became a target for hate after contacting tenants of a building owned by Sherry Spencer, warning them about possible protests over Richard Spencer's views. When Sherry Spencer called to ask her advice, Gersh said, she advised her to sell the building and donate money to a human rights group as a way to defuse tensions, adding that she offered to help Spencer sell the property (Simon, 2018). After a public blog, written by Sherry Spencer, accusing Gersh of threatening her livelihood, and stating that Gersh had told her that protesters and media would turn up and drive down the building's value if she didn't sell, Anglin started writing about it on the *Daily Stormer*. He encouraged 'his troll army to tell Gersh what they thought of her and on his website he posted her personal information and ways to reach her' (Simon, 2018). Most of the messages contained hate-filled language, centering on the fact that Gersh is Jewish, and containing extreme antisemitic images. Gersh said she received voice mails with the sound of gunshots, together with mass vile antisemitism, including references to her son and a gas oven, and images of Gersh and her son and Auschwitz. Anglin claimed it was all free speech protected by the First Amendment.

The second element in this history of the alt-right is what Anglin (2016) refers to as 'conspiracy theorism' that, throughout the 00s, was a key dissident movement on the internet. It gained traction 'initially with theories surrounding the 9/11 attacks having been orchestrated by intelligence agencies'. This was connected to the term 'New World Order', as well as 'more obscure theories regarding Freemasonry and global satanism'. At the turn of the decade, he explains, conspiracy theorists became increasingly focused on what he refers to as 'the Jewish problem' (Anglin, 2016).

Third, Anglin (2016) describes how, in the early 2010s, many in the libertarian community turned to fascism and national socialism 'as competing alternatives to the current system of materialism, consumerism and corrupt crony capitalism'.

Fourth, consistent with fascism's male supremacist cult of masculinity, rampant sexism, and misogyny (see chapter 1, p. 12 of this book) there is the 'manosphere', 'groups of men disillusioned with feminism in society'. 'Having used the starting point of feminism to look at the ills of our modern society', Anglin (2016) states, 'many of these men began to look at the Jews (who happened to have invented feminism) as playing a destructive role in the development of modern Western culture'. 'Already outside of the bounds of what is socially acceptable', he informs us, 'these guys did not have a problem entering into new realms of political incorrectness' (Anglin, 2016). David Neiwert (2017) describes the manosphere as 'an open sewer of rampant misogyny and rape culture, particularly at the "Men's Rights Activists" (or MRA) discussion boards at 4chan'. 'Within this world', he goes on, 'MRAs called feminism "a social cancer,"' and asserted that "Feminism is a hate movement designed to disenfranchise and dehumanize men". These men 'complained that women "cry rape" too easily, and, using Holocaust denialism as a metaphor [the Nazis created 'Jewish conspiracy' to justify mass slaughter], claimed that feminists had "created" the concept of patriarchy to justify abortion and "the destruction of men and masculinity"' (Southern Poverty Law Center, 2012, cited in Neiwert, 2017).

'Given the various communities gathering at 4chan', Neiwert (2017) argues, 'it was unsurprising . . . all these forces converged to create the "Gamergate" controversy', the fifth of Anglin's (2016) elements in this history of the alt-right – 'an initially online phenomenon that crept over into the real world' Neiwert (2017). 'Gamergate' was a bitter online dispute in 2014 that revolved around the internal politics of the video-gaming community. As Neiwert elucidates, on one side there were feminists and other progressive people who argued for greater inclusion of games appealing to women. On the other were men who found such talk not merely threatening but a declaration of a 'culture war' wherein, from their perspective, 'social justice warriors' (SJWs – a generic alt-right term for all those who campaign for social justice) used the cudgel of political correctness to impose the values of multiculturalism.

Neiwert (2017) continues, the mostly white men making these arguments were not content merely to debate their positions online. Instead, 'a whole army of them swung into action on social media and Internet chat rooms, harassing and threatening feminists and liberals'. One of the feminists' leading assailants, Milo Yiannopoulos, described the anti-Gamergate faction as 'an army of sociopathic feminist programmers and campaigners, abetted by achingly politically correct American tech bloggers, [who] are terrorising the entire community – lying, bullying and manipulating their way around the internet for profit and attention' (cited in Neiwert, 2017). These anti-feminist video game players turned to what is now the alt-right in the 10s (Anglin, 2016).

Anglin (2016) concludes his history of the alt-right by noting that these five constituencies combined to various degrees with the older white nationalist movements that have been around since the 1950s. As he points out, these tend to be older men in a movement that is mainly composed of millennials (Anglin, 2016).

In a comment that pertains to Mann's (2004, 13–14) 'statism' feature of fascism, namely the need for an authoritarian leader (see chapter 1, p. 11 of this book), Anglin stresses that, because of the fact that there is not yet an official doctrine, the alt-right movement is 'entirely leaderless'. Although, there are 'minor leaders', 'no actual leader exists' and the 'mob is the movement' (Anglin, 2016).

Propaganda and ideology of the alt-right

The detail presented above would suggest a process of mutual interlocking reinforcements of hatred for other human beings, based on prejudices of the worst kind. Not so, to Anglin, who claims that these various people eventually arrived at the alt-right as a result of their search for 'objective truth'. For Anglin, his is the reason these different groups 'ended up coming to the same conclusions about the Jews, race, feminism and the rest of it', having had 'unlimited access to information, and open minds' (Anglin, 2016). Does Anglin really believe this, or is it merely his cover for neo-Nazi propaganda?

Whereas for Hitler (1925–6), by far 'the most effective branch of political education . . . "propaganda"' was carried on by the Press . . . 'a kind of school for adults', for Anglin and his followers, public pedagogies of hate and for fascism *at the present conjuncture* are perpetrated for the most part on the internet. One can confidently assume that Anglin has read and understood the implications of the following quote from his mentor:

> Propaganda has as little to do with science as an advertisement poster has to do with art . . . The purpose of propaganda is not the personal instruction of the individual, but rather to attract public attention to certain things, the importance of which can be brought home to the masses only by this means. Here the art of propaganda consists in putting a matter so clearly and forcibly before the minds of the people as to create a general conviction regarding the reality of a certain

fact, the necessity of certain things and the just character of something that is essential . . . its purpose must be exactly that of the advertisement poster, to attract the attention of the masses and not by any means to dispense individual instructions to those who already have an educated opinion on things or who wish to form such an opinion on grounds of objective study – because that is not the purpose of propaganda, it must appeal to the feelings of the public rather than to their reasoning powers . . . all effective propaganda must be confined to a few bare essentials and those must be expressed as far as possible in stereotyped formulas. These slogans should be persistently repeated until the very last individual has come to grasp the idea that has been put forward.

(Hitler, 1925–6)

Addressing the ideology and values of the alt-right, Anglin states that they 'are reactionary, formed in opposition to the modern Jewish norms', and lists in addition to antisemitism and the creation of a white ethno-state (already discussed):

- 'scientific racism' [the belief that so-called 'races' have vastly different abilities, drives, and intelligence levels]. This has been repeatedly debunked by scholarly research (Evans, 2018);
- opposition to feminism and gender equality ('sending women back to the home to produce and raise children, largely removing them from the workplace' and against 'homosexuality, as well as the emasculation of men through denying them their traditional role in society');
- endorsement of White History (viewing white people 'as the creators and maintainers of Western civilization');
- cultural normalization ('using authoritarian measures to deal with addictive drugs, pornography, crime and other degenerate social ills');
- common sense economics ('technological developments have made economic issues much less relevant' but 'economics should follow basic common sense');
- the white struggle as a global battle against Jews (Anglin, 2016).

Anglin has also given his views on LGBT issues elsewhere. According to Luke O'Brien (2017), senior reporter at *HuffPost*, Anglin has 'advocated, for instance, throwing gays off buildings, isis-style' (O'Brien, 2017). Spencer Sunshine (2017), associate fellow at Political Research Associates, has pointed out that homophobic and transphobic statements are the norm in the alt-right, and at Charlottesville, 'fascists chanted repeatedly at anti-racist protestors, "Fuck you faggots".'[6] With respect to popular culture and everyday life, it is the alt-right's view that both exclude and denigrate straight white men, and that the dominant discourse is against them.

As Sunshine (2017) points out 'Antifa' now often takes the place of the Soviet Union as the agent of conspiracy. As with other questions, however, he goes on, some central alt-right figures have a more favorable view of the Soviet Union and other similar states as they actually existed, rather than as they portrayed themselves in the abstract. Matthew Heimbach and others, he states, praise North Korea as an ethno-state that practices national socialism (Sunshine, 2017). Could it be that Trump has become aware of this, and could this be why he has subsequently warmed to Kim Jong-un?

Anglin goes on to stress the importance to the alt-right of memes, the most prominent of which is 'Pepe' the cartoon frog, appropriated by the alt-right as a racist and antisemitic amphibian (Segal, 2016). As he puts it, for a movement that 'meets all of the SPLC's definitions of Neo-Nazi White Supremacism, using a cartoon frog to represent itself takes on a subversive power to bypass historical stereotypes of such movements'. Some of the other significant alt-right memes include 'Bane', who embodies the 'Jewish nightmare of fascism' and therefore is a hero to the alt-right; 'Dindu Nuffin', used to mock black people; 'shitlord' (a term of endearment and pride); 'Le Happy Merchant' ('portraying Jews as an alien other', in similar ways to the NSDAP (German Nazi Party)); 'holo-hoax' (even 'if it had happened, it would have been justified')[7]; nirvana fallacy ('designed to mock the ridiculousness of the liberal/progressive/ SJW[Social Justice Warrior]/Jew assertion that all races are exactly the same') (Anglin, 2016). There are also 'cute cartoon girls wearing various kinds of Nazi regalia, or sporting openly misogynistic, racist and antisemitic texts' (Neiwert, 2017).

'The end goal of the Alt-Right', Anglin (2016) asserts:

> is to first solidify a stable and self-sustaining counter-culture, and then eventually push this into becoming the dominant culture, in the same way that the Jewish-led revolutionary counter-culture of the 1960s has now become the dominant culture of the West.

Anglin has an 'interesting' take on Trump's alleged 'shithole countries' remark, a snippet of public pedagogy that might turn out to be, like Charlottesville in 2017, a major turning point for the alt-right (Charlottesville being the event that will be remembered as the year neo-Nazis 're-emerged as a visible presence in the United States and the word alt-right became a common household term': Maza, 2017). Adam Lusher (2018) writes, 'While most of the world recoils in horror, neo-Nazis celebrate the presidents reported remarks as "encouraging and refreshing" because "it indicates Trump is more or less on the same page as us with regards to race and immigration".' (Anglin, 2018 in the *Daily Stormer*, cited in Lusher, 2018). Anglin had one slight reservation, namely that Trump had reportedly suggested he might accept Asian immigrants because they would help the US economically: 'Yes, he said the thing about Asian countries, which shows that he is not actually a racist and is instead concerned about merit, but that is a huge leap from where the rest of the entirety of the political system in this country is at'. (Anglin, 2018, cited in Lusher, 2018). Anglin added that Trump:

> may have just made the comment about Asians so as to not seem racist.[8] I think it is clear that Trump's ideal America is the one he grew up with in the 1950s. And the closer we get to that, the closer we are to our own goals of a white race-state.
>
> (cited in Lusher, 2018)

In addition, Duke noted:

> Just as the most ardent Trump supporters were about to give up on him in despair, he restores a lot of love in us by saying blunt but truthful things that no other President in our lifetime would dare say! NO DACA! NO COMPROMISE – NO Sh**thole America! Hail Trump!
>
> (cited in Lusher, 2018)

As noted in chapter 2, it was reported that Trump suggested that he would prefer Norwegian immigrants to those from Africa or Haiti. Consequently, Spencer changed his Twitter handle to include the Norwegian flag, pinning a tweet stating:

> I must come to the defense of Haiti! It's a potentially beautiful and productive country. The problem is that it's filled with shithole people. If the French dominated, they could make it great again. #MakeHaitiGreatAgain

Spencer's views on sending ships to provide humanitarian aid after a hurricane in Haiti in 2017 are that the ships should have been sent to enslave Haitians instead: 'You should go enslave them. That would actually be a proper war aim' (cited in Holt, 2018). Spencer then apologized for 'really going nuts' before retracting the apology, and adding, 'you need to go nuts in order to prove a point' (cited in Holt, 2018). He said he hoped white people in America get so frustrated with the military's humanitarian efforts that they 'flip over into this domineering type, and I obviously hope that happens' (cited in Holt, 2018):

> This is the kind of thing that's truly traditional and historical. You display your power. Phallic symbols in the center of the capital city. That's what it's all fucking about.
>
> (cited in Holt, 2018)

He also lamented that the United States military never engages in war 'for the right reasons' which he said are when 'you want to dominate someone, you want to take their territory, you want to take their women' And if those reasons don't suffice, Spencer believes it is acceptable to go to war simply for 'vainglory' (cited in Holt, 2018):

The far-right commentator Paul Kersey was also enthusiastic about Trump's 'shithole' comments, stating on his 'Stuff Black People Don't Like' website:

> The 'shithole' comment by Donald Trump has been his most illuminating and beautiful moment as President of the United States, helping punctuate how the corporate/mainstream/legacy media exists to run public relations for the very people turning much of America into a 'shithole' as well.
>
> (cited in Lusher, 2018)

Kersey went on:

> We live in the early stages of revolutionary times, where the restoration of racial sanity seems plausible. Who knew the entire anti-white world order was so fragile [that] the uttering of one adjective – to describe the conditions non-whites collectively create in the absence of white people – was [enough] to blow away decades of carefully-crafted plans to convince whites they had a moral duty to set aside the dreams of their people to uplift the lives of every other person on the planet?
>
> (cited in Lusher, 2018)

Kersey once said of black people, 'They know that White people are superior. They whine about it all the time and want to kill us because of it. They know they come from jungle savages and will never be equal to us so they destroy everything we create' (cited in Stern, 2016.

Whereas Trump's public pedagogy may be viewed as contained *within* Giroux's (2010) 'public pedagogy of hate', though with a fair amount of fascist(ic) intent, that of the alt-right is one step beyond it, in that it aims to be more educative, though abusive and offensive too, with much of it painful to repeat. I do so, lest there be any doubt as to the nature of the public pedagogy that the alt-right is attempting to spew out.

Christopher Cantwell: the dialectic of fascism personified

Christopher Cantwell used the Charlottesville rally as a major platform for public pedagogy for fascism. Filmed close-up by Vice News (2017) fervently chanting the aforementioned slogan 'Jews will not replace us' at the rally, he was later interviewed by correspondent Elle Reeve. Cantwell offered racist critiques of black and Jewish people and confirmed that alt-right was violent, defending the killing of Heather Heyer as 'justified'. At one point in the interview, Cantwell stated, I'm carrying a pistol, I go to the gym all the time, I'm trying to make myself more capable of violence' (Mark, 2017b). Later Cantwell said he hoped for a leader who was 'a lot more racist than Donald Trump' and, true to his fascist beliefs, compounding antisemitism with sexism, while referring to the marriage between Trump's daughter Ivanka and Jared Kushner, who 'does not give his daughter to a Jew' (Vice News, 2017): 'I don't think that you could feel about race the way that I do and watch that Kushner bastard walk around with that beautiful girl, OK?'

Later he anticipated that 'a lot more people are going to die before we're done here':

This is part of the reason that we want an ethno-state. The blacks are killing each other in staggering numbers from coast to coast – we don't really want a part of that anymore, and so the fact that they resist us when we say we want a homeland is not shocking to me. These people want violence, and the right is just meeting a market demand.

(Mark, 2017b)

At the end of the video, posing next to a computer monitor with a swastika prominently on display, Cantwell revealed how he came to the rally heavily armed, tossing on to his hotel bed an AK rifle, three handguns and a knife, and informing Reeve that he had another AK in another part of the room, that was then picked up by the camera (Vice News, 2017).

Recalling Renton's discussion of the dialectic of fascism: a mass movement (in Cantwell's case, the attempt to build such a movement) and a reactionary ideology (see chapter 1, pp. 12–13 of this book), Christopher Cantwell is not just a street-fighting Nazi (a prime example of Mann's 2004, 16 'bottom-up paramilitarism' feature of fascism: see chapter 1, p. 12 of this book), but also spreads his public pedagogy for fascism on his call-in talk show, 'Radical Agenda'. Cantwell says he receives the most referrals to his show from the *Daily Stormer*. Guests include the aforementioned (endnote 6 of this chapter) Matthew Heimbach; Augustus Invictus (a violent second civil war is needed to preserve 'Western Civilization');[9] and Andrew 'Weev' Auernheimer (who has threatened that Jewish children will be slaughtered).[10] 'Radical Agenda' is live-streamed via Facebook and UStream. Cantwell also makes use of many of the same dark memes as other alt-right supporters, both on his show and on his Facebook page. Some praise Pinochet (Southern Poverty Law Center – SPLC, 2017), whose political opponents were ejected from helicopters (Franklin, 2001). At Charlottesville, Cantwell was wearing a t-shirt embroidered with a picture of 'communists' being thrown out of a helicopter (Vice News, 2017). According to Cantwell, Democrats and 'communists' need to be 'physically removed' from the US and white men should consider polygamy to increase number of 'Caucasian' babies being born, his goal being to 'normalize racism', combined with a belief that Jews have to die (SPLC, 2017).

On chemical and biological weapons, he has stated that they 'can do a great deal of good for mankind. Releasing nerve gas or some kind of lethal virus into a left-wing protest could prepare the bodies for physical removal without making a big scene for the cameras or destroying anything of value' (Facebook post, January 28, 2017, cited in SPLC, 2017). As far as immigration is concerned, Cantwell has stated:

> It's the right thing to be concerned about the immigration, because you see these fucking hordes of unwashed religious fanatics pouring across borders with no resources just thinking that they're going to collect welfare and fuck our women and fucking breed us out of existence. That makes me want to bash people's skulls open.
>
> (Interviewed on The Daily Shoah,
> September 22, 2015, cited in SPLC, 2017)

With a history of hatred for the state, and, in particular the police, Cantwell's focus has shifted away from the police to Jews, blacks, and leftists, and has stated, 'I don't think there's an honest person in America who doesn't think that the reason blacks are filling up our prisons is because they are dumber than us' (cited in SPLC, 2017). Cantwell has no problem calling for all Jews to be 'gassed' largely because he sees Jewish people as agents of 'communism' (SPLC, 2017).[11] Unsurprisingly, Cantwell is still a supporter of Trump, even though he would like him to be more racist and practice anti-semitism. Trump enables some of Cantwell's fantasies involving Trump's deputizing 'Right Wing Death Squads' and issuing 'communist hunting license by executive order' (one of Cantwell's Facebook posts, cited in SPLC, 2017). Cantwell is currently under house arrest in Virginia on two felony charges for allegedly using tear gas and pepper spray at the Charlottesville rally (Hayden, 2018).

Conclusion

In this chapter, I began with a brief examination of the political and economic backdrop to the ascendancy of Donald J. Trump and the alt-right. I moved on to an analysis of the public pedagogy for fascism of some of the latter's key figures. In the next chapter, I address three internet sites that aim to promote public pedagogies for fascism. In the final two chapters of the book, I turn my attention to progressive resistance and revolution.

Notes

1 Peter McLaren, from comments on an earlier draft of this book.
2 For a full analysis of those who voted for Trump, see BBC News (2016).
3 For an alternative (neo-) Marxist interpretation of the history of the United States, see Cole (2016, Chapter 2).
4 My focus in this chapter is on the alt-right in the US. However, a report by UK-based anti-fascist and anti-racist advocacy group, HOPE not hate (2017) shows that close links are being made between North America and Europe. Jason Reza Jorjani, a founder, along with Spencer and others, of the AltRight Corporation, an organization established to foster cooperation and coordination among alt-right groups in Europe and North America, has stated: 'we will have a Europe, in 2050, where the bank notes have Adolf Hitler . . . he is just going to be seen as a great European leader' (cited in Singal, 2017).
5 Alpesh Maisuria (2016, 92) has demonstrated how humor can also be used to promote a socialist agenda, giving British organic intellectual, Russell Brand as an example: 'Brand skilfully uses irreverence to do serious critical work, and this method resonates with the culture and language of the masses, particularly the British youth who deploy irony and sarcasm in every speech talk and action'.
6 Sunshine (2017) points out that it is not totally straightforward. For example, *Fascism Today* author Shane Burley said in an email, 'The hardcore homophobia is actually kind of new for the Alt Right, it wasn't an area of importance for quite a while. It essentially returned when the less academic voices in the Alt Right came back and the queer voices receded, like Jack Donovan' (cited in Sunshine, 2017). Donovan self-describes as an *androphile* – a man whose love of masculinity includes sex with other men (see O'Connor, 2017 for further explanation). At the 2016 National Policy Institute (discussed later in this chapter) conference, 'the most pro-GLBTQ strain was on display' and Donovan spoke. Matthew Heimbach, leader of the neo-Nazi Traditionalist Worker Party, ant-abortion, anti-gay marriage, anti-immigration and advocate for a white ethno-state with women staying in the home, was banned from attending due to his aggressive homophobic approach, and longtime White nationalist lawyer Sam Dickson made the amazing statement that "gay people" will be allowed in the new White ethnostate' (Sunshine, 2017).
7 The most offensive 'joke' about the Holocaust I have come across is from Heimbach. He told writer and journalist Tony Rehagen, during a meal at Pizza Hut,

'*Mein Kampf* is a good book that makes some good points. I was so disappointed. I read the whole book and there was no plan to kill 6 million Jews in it. It was like, "Did they take that part out?"' Rehagen adds, 'No one laughs' (Rehagen, 2017). Before Charlottesville, Heimbach said a Jewish conspiracy was behind the removal of Confederate memorials, because 'they want to be able to destroy knowledge of the past so they, the Jewish Power Structure, can try and control the future' (cited in Sunshine, 2017).

 8 It may be for the same reason that Trump commended lower unemployment rates for African Americans and 'Hispanics' when addressing the anti-abortion rally in January, 2018: see chapter 1, endnote 9. In reality, these lower rates are part of an ongoing trend, rather than a Trump 'achievement' (Lockhart, 2018; White, 2018).

 9 See Southern Poverty Law Center (SPSC) (undated).

10 See Lydia Smith (2018).

11 Communism is a greatly misunderstood term, and generally refers in common usage (inaccurately) to the Soviet Union and Eastern European countries in the Stalin era. It is outside the scope of this book to consider the possibilities of creating communism, as envisaged by Karl Marx's co-writer, Freiderich Engels (although Engels attributed the underlying concept to Marx). In Anti-Dühring, Engels (1955) referred to a form of existence beyond socialism, when the state will have 'withered away', and we will all live communally. Rikowski (2018), however, has argued that communism exists as a suppressed form of life in capitalist society. Furthermore, Rikowski claims that capitalism's existence and development are dependent on the vibrancy of communism as an already existing societal foundation for capitalism, principally in terms of the social production and reproduction of labor power in schools, families, and other institutions) (Rikowski, 2018). Elsewhere (Rikowski, forthcoming, 2019) he has expanded the point, suggesting that that while these institutions perform this crucial role in the maintenance and continuation of capitalism, the processes they enable cannot be separated from 'the love, kindness and solidarity involved in rearing and nurturing children and young people and having a concern for their development in a loving manner'. He concludes, 'These feelings of love, solidarity, kindness etc. for children can also be extended to our adult lives in our struggles for a better society, a better world – and this is the communist impulse in action' (Rikowski, forthcoming, 2019). Socialist Parties and their vision for socialism in the US, and its feasibility in more general terms are discussed in chapter 6 of this book.

4 'The_Donald'; 'Trump-like candidates in the future'; and 'waking up whites from their slumber' – public pedagogy furthering the fascist agenda

Introduction

In this chapter, I demonstrate the fundamental role of social media in facilitating the lurch towards mainstream fascism, by an examination of three major alt-right organs of public pedagogy, first a Reddit (an American social news aggregation) known as The_Donald, aimed at various constituencies of men and boys who support Trump and also share a fascination for the internet as a means to spread offense and hatred. Second, I consider the National Policy Institute, aimed squarely at the male academic community and seeking policy initiatives for fascist power. Third, I look at the (US) official alt-right website, targeting male academics and other well-educated men and promoting neo-Nazism. As is the case with traditional fascism, there is a dialectical relationship between the alt-right's ideological core (Renton, 1999, 3), as discussed in chapter 1 of this book (see pp. 12–13), and its existence as a movement, both on the internet and on the streets, of which, with respect to the latter, Charlottesville was a milestone.

/r/The_Donald: breeding ground for the alt-right

/r/The_Donald is a Reddit community with over half a million subscribers, and a breeding ground for the alt-right. As Tim Squirrell (2017) puts it, it is 'the fermenting vat in which this identity is being formed'. According to Alexa (2018) Reddit is the fourth most visited site in the US, after Google, YouTube, and Facebook. Squirrell (2017) interrogated a collection of every Reddit comment made – 3 billion – discovering a number of distinct alt-right constituencies that share different opinions and ways to express them, distinguishable by the language they use and the communities they post in. There is thus what he describes as 'a taxonomy of trolls' (Squirrell, 2017). Squirrell (2017) identified five groups on /r/The_Donald: the 'The4chan shitposters'; the 'anti-progressive gamers'; 'men's rights activists'; 'white supremacists;' and 'anti-globalists'. I will discuss each in turn.

The 4chan shitposters

The 4chan shitposters provoke offense and outrage, often using extreme racist, sexist, and antisemitic slurs. As Squirrell (2017) explains, you cannot argue with them because any attempt at a serious conversation is met by a plea of 'only joking!' They talk about memes such as Pepe the Frog; 'Kikistan' (a fictional country of disparate and dispossessed people, the country of origin of the shitposters); and 'normies' (boring conventional and mainstream people), whom they despise. The most common words used by these trolls are 'kek' (someone from Kikistan); Pepe; and 'deus vult' (in Latin, 'God wills it', a battle cry of the Crusaders). Another common word is 'tendies'. True to fascism's disablism (see chapter 1, p. 19), tendies stories feature a twenty-something autistic man who lives with his mother and keeps demanding chicken tenders in exchange for 'good boy points' he earns by doing chores and taking care of himself. He terrorizes his parents and frequently complains about normies (Know Your Meme, 2018). 4chan shitposters frequently refer to Trump as 'God Emperor' (Beal, 2018) (hence Anglin's response to Trump's election victory, referred to in chapter 3 of this book).

Anti-progressive gamers

Anti-progressive gamers despise 'social-justice warriors' (SJW) (a pejorative term for people who promote social justice), LGBT communities, and feminists, believing that major film and game studios are pandering to these hated people by such events as all-female screenings of *Wonder Woman* (Squirrell, 2017). They are transphobic, repeating the words, 'there are only two genders' constantly. Some common words used by anti-progressive gamers are SJW; 'snowflake' (a term for someone who thinks they are unique and special, but really are not); pandering; feminist; and 'virtue signalling' (a slur for a member of the so-called liberal elite, yet another euphemistic slur: an educated person of influence who disagrees with you) (Gold, 2017).

Men's rights activists

This group campaigns for men's rights in custody battles and workplace deaths, but also includes various types of anti-feminists and misogynists. Some are 'involuntary celibates', who want to have sex or find a partner but are not able to – and blame women for this. Others are 'Men Going Their Own Way', who believe that they can find true liberation in what they perceive to be a female-dominated world only by refusing to interact with women completely (Squirrell, 2017). Woman are referred to as 'females', and men they perceive as weak are called 'cucks' (Squirrell, 2017). Other words used often here are 'bitch'; 'alpha' (a male who gets all the sex he wants); chad (the archetypal alpha bad boy); 'beta' (a man who doesn't get enough sex); and 'omega' (a man at the bottom of the sexual hierarchy who has no prospect of sex at all) (Squirrell, 2017).

White supremacists

Squirrell (2017) ponders that it might seem surprising that the language of white supremacy is quite uncommon in The_Donald. This is because *explicit* racism is banned. Implicit or coded racism, however, is very common, for example with people displaying Islamophobic sentiment and passing it off as criticizing Islamism, or claiming that 'Islam is not compatible with Western culture'. White supremacists also populate other sites like The Daily Stormer and Stormfront (another neo-Nazi website). The most common words used by the white supremacists include 'Islam'; '(creeping) Sharia'; 'deus vult'; 'western culture', along with the various racial slurs that they can get away with.

Anti-globalists

Anti-globalists believe in conspiracy theories, particularly that anyone who opposes Trump's agenda must disagree with his premise that America's interests come first, and is therefore part of some sort of global conspiracy to overthrow American power (Shapiro, 2016). They are interested in news about 'bad things' perpetrated by members of minority groups and left-wing people) (Squirrell, 2017). As Squirrell puts it, 'Their hyperbolic conspiratorial language might sound absurd, but it's become an increasingly coherent and important part of The_Donald'. Among their most common words are 'globalist scum'; 'the establishment', 'puppets', 'elites', 'masters' and 'cultural Marxist'.

This last term merits a little wider explanation than the other widely used words on The_Donald, since 'cultural Marxism' enjoys a wide currency among the alt-right. As Jason Wilson (2015) argues, it is a flexible phrase 'that can be tailored to fit with the obsessions of a range of right-wing actors'. For the alt-right, 'cultural Marxism' is invoked for whatever they disapprove of, such as the various constituencies of 'enemies' discussed so far. Moreover, from the alt-right's perspective, 'political correctness', a misnomer for respect for other peoples' identities (see chapter 1, endnote 8), is a product of 'cultural Marxism' (Wilson, 2015), and thus hated by the alt-right and its fellow travelers.

According to the alt-right and other neo-fascist groups, 'cultural Marxism' represents a 'master plan' for the overthrow of Western civilization from within, personified by those members of the Frankfurt School – Jewish-German academics – who fled Nazi Germany in 1936 and moved to New York (Oliver, 2017). The 'theory' of 'cultural Marxism', as ideologically fabricated by the alt-right, is thus essentially antisemitic, with a longer history than Marxism (Wilson, 2015), and forms part of a belief in a Jewish conspiracy theory, whereby Jewish people are involved in an ongoing secret plot to take over the whole world.

Before killing 77 people in 2011, the Norwegian far-right extremist Anders Behring Breivik had electronically circulated a tract protesting against what he saw as 'the rise of cultural Marxism/multiculturalism in the West' (Oliver, 2017).[1] For the alt-right, American society has already been taken over by 'cultural Marxism', which, as Oliver (2017) argues, they believe is responsible for:

> Queer Studies, globalisation, bad modern art, women wanting a life on top of babymaking, African-American Studies, the 1960s, post-structuralism: essentially, everything that isn't nationalist, 'white' and Christian.

The hatred of Marxists by traditional fascists has been usurped by the hatred of '*cultural* Marxists' by neo-fascists.

Squirrell (2017) sums up his analysis of The_Donald, as follows. For a long time, these people would have very limited reason to interact with one another, since there was not 'much in common between meme aficionados, gamers, sexists, conspiracy theorists, and racists'. However, with the advent of the era of Trump they have started to use public pedagogy to coalesce, and are communicating in, and developing and evolving, their own unique language, as well as re-interpreting and amending existing language.

One word used in The_Donald is particularly significant – 'cuck'. As noted earlier, it refers to 'weak men'. It is a shortening of 'cuckold', an old word 'used to refer to men who allow their [female] partners to sleep with other men (and often find sexual gratification in the humiliation of it)'. Its use, Squirrell (2017) points out, 'has become the *sine qua non* of alt-right group membership'. It is used in multiple senses, such as: 'cuckservative' used to describe 'conservatives who are seen as being too soft and allowing their countries (primarily European) to be "invaded" by Islam and Muslims'; 'libcuck'; 'cuckbook;' 'starcucks' and 'cuck Schumer' (Senate Minority Leader Chuck Schumer) to refer to 'liberal' things generally. One more usage of 'cuck' is worth mentioning: 'when anyone who *isn't* the alt-right uses it to mock those who *do* use it, flipping its meaning entirely'. 'As a result', Squirrell (2017) stresses, 'it's everywhere'.

Squirrell (2017) concludes his analysis of the dangers of this aspect of the pro-Trump lobby as follows:

> The_Donald and other alt-right spaces are acting as meeting places for disaffected white men from all walks of life to share a communal hatred. They start out in different corners of the internet with different interests and different lexicons. They remain separate when they're outside of The_Donald, but the more time they spend in there, the more pernicious views of the world they are likely to pick up by osmosis. They are forming a coherent group identity, represented in the language they have begun to speak, which coalesces around their common hatred of liberalism and their love of Donald Trump.

Hence bored teenagers and gamers are, right before our eyes, 'becoming indoctrinated into hard-line anti-globalism . . . *on a publicly accessible forum*' (my emphasis) (Squirrell, 2017). The_Donald thus epitomizes *par excellence* an established and growing public pedagogy of hate. In addition, with its rampant racism, antisemitism, and accompanying belief in Jewish conspiracy theory, together with its Islamophobia and dedication to white supremacy, alongside its sexism, misogyny, and uncompromising anti-feminism and contempt for women, the site represents a (potential) burgeoning public pedagogy for fascism.

The_Donald is complemented by the National Policy Institute, whose president is Richard Spencer, and the alt-right official website (Spencer founded the alt-right, as we have seen). Unlike The_Donald, though, both the National Policy Institute and the website are aimed primarily at an academic audience (Spencer self-describes as a 'dissident intellectual' [Ruptly, 2017]). I will consider each in turn.

The National Policy Institute: preparing policy for its goal of neo-fascist power

With the aim of fleshing out the National Policy Institute (NPI)'s vision of a neo-fascist/neo-Nazi future, at the end of 2017 its executive director, Evan McLaren, in language typical of the academy, issued a 'call for papers'. The call's title is 'Putting the Policy in the National Policy Institute', and begins with the following statement: 'To understand the need for a new vision and program for national policy, one need only reflect on the candidacy and administration of Donald Trump' (NPI, 2017). The call for papers is aimed at 'nationalist-minded people . . . affected by a deeper concern for the condition and fate of our civilization, and for individuals who long felt their voices stifled by an oppressive atmosphere of political correctness.'

The call describes 'Trump's drive through the 2016 presidential campaign as entertaining and often inspiring. At his best, Trump represents the renewed energy and sense of possibility that would ignite our collective revival as a serious people with both a past and a future' (NPI, 2017).

However, it goes on, Trump 'was always a little inscrutable, possibly shallow, and often reckless', and is never able to accomplish his governmental project without help. Trump, it concludes, needs capable people who relate to his radical instincts and ambition, and who can define and intelligently defend his program . . . and prepare it for the new direction towards which he had pointed throughout his campaign (NPI, 2017). There follows a section entitled, 'Challenging Conservatism, Inc. and Liberalism, LLC'. Conservatism, it argues, 'has long drawn criticism for its effect and apparent design as a channel to divert the energies and anxieties of white peoples into harmless and irrelevant discourses of thought and patterns of political action'. 'Ultimately', it concludes, 'conservatism has failed to conserve anything of value' (NPI, 2017). Liberalism, on the other hand, 'consists of appeals to ethereal notions of fairness and equality couched in a comprehensive grammar of white self-hatred and intolerance', and 'is now totally absorbed by white guilt-feeling and bounded by the vocabulary arising from it' (NPI, 2017). It concludes:

> Together, institutionalized Conservatism and Liberalism act to police the marketplace of ideas and monopolize its thought-franchises. In order to enter politics with any hope of influencing policy in or outside of government, one must brand as 'liberal' or 'conservative' and maintain informal certifications from corresponding policy institutions that enjoy many millions of dollars of support. Those who step outside of this perimeter are labeled morally ill and quasi-genocidal and are excluded from respectable society. The result is a policy establishment that wholly forbids white peoples from forming serious concepts of their civilizational identity and self-belonging. Every idea advanced by this establishment is harmful to the prospects of white survival and prosperity. With no more than a handful of possible exceptions, Donald Trump was obliged to staff his administration with people approved by this establishment, and who in many cases made their livelihood from and within it.
>
> (NPI, 2017)

This 'bipartite establishment has been dominant for so long that nationalist, racially-minded white people have learned to accept it as a fixed reality' and many 'have totally despaired of the potential for an awakened white consciousness again animating national governance' (NPI, 2017). There then follows a bid for political power from the NPI, which is described as 'a beachhead against the political establishment' (NPI, 2017):

> The National Policy Institute rejects this despair. White peoples will reawaken to their own shared identity and reconnect with their common past and future. They will do so because, in order to secure their own existence, they must. To succeed, white peoples must direct their effort and energy at institutions and seats of power . . . [with] the goal of civilization-wide renewal. To overcome obstacles in Washington, D.C., we must go through them. We must outline real policy, articulating its fundamental purposes and describing it down to its gritty details. We must relentlessly professionalize and make certain that, when Trump-like candidates and contingencies arise in the future, they have a comprehensive script from which to read and a serious professional infrastructure on which to rely. In turn, our activity and inspiring vision will lead more such candidates to step forward in the first place.

The specified areas for the papers that will be published by NPI (minimum 3,000 words; Chicago style of citation) and which can be either 'formal proposals for government action on a particular issue' or an 'information paper [that] provides information on a particular topic but does not make any formal policy recommendations' are:

- the crisis of white civilization and the geopolitical ideal of the ethnostate
- white erasure in the Third World and the necessity of a new colonialism
- the dilemma of dual Israeli/U.S. citizenship and Jewish/White identity
- the posture of the West towards Russia
- the conflict in the Ukraine
- the U.S.'s approach to the Middle East
- the white genocide in South Africa
- the limits of ethnonationalism
- the meaning and fate of Brexit
- the need for remigration
- reform in collegiate athletics
- the case for student debt amnesty
- the failure of egalitarian education reform
- the need for well-funded public transportation
- the case for nationalized healthcare
- the internet censorship emergency
- environmentalism and conservation
- the costs of diversity
- the reality and future of genetic research

- the opioid crisis and the White Death
- family, marriage, and divorce, and the need for a national program of natalism.

(NPI, 2017)

The National Policy Institute's 'call for papers' is nothing less than a plea for neo-fascist/neo-Nazi public intellectuals to contribute to the creation of a neo-fascist/neo-Nazi public pedagogy in preparation for the NPI's dream of a fascist America.

The alt-right website: heralding the beginning of a new racially defined America

The alt-right's public pedagogical aims are clearly revealed by an article appearing on its website late in 2017. Written in academic language by a 'guest writer', it is an attempt to link 'public intellectualism' (the development of (neo-) fascist theory) with social activism (a 'racially' aware grassroots movement). It begins with a quote from *Francis Parker Yockey*, who from 1946 until his death in a San Francisco jail cell in 1960 was tracked across three continents by the US government, which suspected (correctly) that he had been spreading anti-American propaganda in Occupied Germany and encouraging ex-Nazis to 'stand up' to US authorities. Yockey published *Imperium*, from which the guest writer's quote is taken, in 1947. In the book, described as 'a modern-day *Mein Kampf* for neo-Nazis', the book declares fascism to be 'the Spirit of the Age' (Mostrom, 2017).

For this 'guest writer' (GW), Trump's days as 'God Emperor' are nearing an end, to be replaced by a mass (neo-) fascist movement. As GW puts it:

> [e]ach day Trump lurches closer to becoming another GOP republican, doing everything possible to implement the failed conservative agenda . . . instead of the populist-nationalist agenda that won him the election . . . Instead of championing his populist base, the base seems to be the only thing holding Trump back [from mainstream republicanism]
>
> (Guest Writer (GW), 2017).

GW (2017) continues:

> Whether Trump continues down the path of total betrayal or rights the ship may not ultimately matter. Congress is hopelessly gridlocked, unable to reach any agreement unless it involves supporting Jewish nationalism (Israel and their Middle East wars) or condemning white nationalism. What a coincidence that those are the only two positions that receive unanimous bi-partisan support.

Since 'American "democracy" is crashing', and since the 'GOP controls all three branches of government and cannot achieve a single legislative victory',

GW (2017) poses the question, '[w]hat does this mean for us', given that '[w]e've reached peak America'? At this point, GW reaches for Nazi Yockey, 'one of the greatest American thinkers this nation has ever produced', who argued that 'cultures rise and fall like the life cycles of an organism – infancy, childhood, adolescence, adulthood, old age, and death' and that a 'nation's journey is driven towards producing the adult stage of its high culture, epitomized, and shaped by the "higher man" that encapsulates the spirit of the nation'. Recalling the fascist notion of a 'führer', Trump, he declares 'is the "higher man" of post-WWII American civic nationalism' (GW, 2017):

> He is 'homo Americanus', the fulfillment of the American dream – an entrepreneur, who built things, became a billionaire, married a model wife, became a famous television celebrity, and finally the President. Money, Fame, Pleasure, these are values that American culture worships, all of which were achieved by Donald Trump. This made him the perfect avatar for a movement to Make America Great Again [MAGA], to reclaim the American dream.

However, GW (2017) despairs:

> the dream no longer belongs to the real Americans whose ancestors fought and died to build this nation. The real Dreamers are the children of illegal aliens, the foreigners who violate American sovereignty, the new Americans . . . the most American people are the nonwhite immigrants who just arrived.

GW then refers to the 'erroneous belief that Race is cultural construct, when in fact Culture is a racial construct', and states that '[c]ommon values derive from a common people'. 'MAGA populism', he goes on, 'resonates with Middle America while viscerally enraging nonwhites, bicoastal elites, and liberals who have internalized white guilt'. 'No matter how much Trump implores people of color to join his movement', he concludes, 'they reject his message because it's a message that speaks to whites, not them . . . Trump does not mark the beginning of a civic nationalist resurgence, but the end of it'. (GW, 2017). 'What we're watching unfold at the White House', GW argues, 'is the exciting denouement to the judeo-liberal fabrication that America is an "idea" and not a people'. In a rallying cry for a new (neo-) fascist United States of America, GW (2017) implores:

> Do not dismay though, for the end of propositional America is the beginning of a new racially defined America. The country itself is dying, but the Europeans who fought, bled, and died to build America are more alive than ever. We are the real Americans, the true heirs

of the Founding Fathers, and only now are we becoming aware of who we are.

In a tribute to Trump, GW states 'no man has come close to Trump in waking up whites from their slumber and stoking the flames of racial consciousness'. GW singles out Trump's aforementioned comments on black athletes and on Mexican immigrants:

> The President is at his best when he relies on his instincts because his instincts are that of a normal, red-blooded American. No better example demonstrates this fact than the President's gut-response to black athletes dishonoring the national anthem: 'get that son of a bitch off the field right now'. It's the same gut reaction that initiated the MAGA movement: 'Mexico's not sending us their best, they're bringing crime, they're rapists'.
>
> (GW, 2017)

'A fundamental principle of the Alt-Right', GW tells us, 'is that politics is downstream from Culture. To that end, Trump is a godsend'. As GW (2017) concludes, regaling in a fascist admiration for Trump's demagogy, and for what is left of his ascendancy to God Emperor, his use of Twitter as public pedagogy to both chastise those opposed to fascism and to further polarize the US in the hope of GW for a (neo-) fascist future:

> From the oval office, he may underachieve with the power of his pen, but at the bully pulpit, he can rain down tweets into the heart of liberalism like thunderbolts from Mount Olympus. With each new attack on the judeo-liberal order, the Left overreacts to the affront to their moral supremacy with gnashing of teeth and unhinged threats launched at the President, escalating the polarization of America into implicitly white and anti-white camps . . . . Trump is shattering the false idol of civic nationalism by showing its complete failure to remedy the fundamental racial divide ripping the country apart. Give thanks, for the end of civic nationalism, means the beginning of a new America nationalism, one that is paradoxically rooted in an older, racially aware American identity. We are the future, if America is to have a future.

Conclusion

In the previous three chapters of this book, I have painted a very bleak picture of the United States in the toxic era of Trump. I have examined

Trump's public pedagogy of hate and fascistic leanings that have emboldened and legitimized fascism. I concentrated then on the alt-right, and how this predominantly neo-Nazi grouping has moved closer to the mainstream. In this chapter, I discussed three influential alt-right internet sites used by the alt-right to spread a public pedagogy for fascism. I now move on to resistance and to revolution, by directing my attention to anti-Trump, anti-fascist resistance and to a consideration of those who are advocating a different type of society, not one based on neo-Nazi ideology, but on socialist principles for the twenty-first century.

Note

1 One can only surmise as to any interconnections between the various references to Norway and Norwegian in this book (see pp. 31, 61, 70).

5 'No Trump! No KKK! No fascist USA!'

Reality and resistance

Introduction

In this chapter, which is about reality and resistance, I begin by providing a snapshot of global and US capitalism in 2018, the year of the mid-term elections, a scenario no less depressing than the growth of hatred and fascism, already described throughout the book. I then assess the effects of Trump's policies on the US working class.

Having looked at the reality of the US today, I move on to resistance from the left of the political spectrum. First, I consider the various protests in numerous US cities that have taken place against Trump from 2015 to the present. People have rallied and demonstrated against his rhetoric and in opposition to his policies, his speeches, and his tweets. I go on to assess the current situation within the alt-right, particularly with respect to the *success* of Antifa, a broad coalition of street-based anti-fascists that also uses the internet, in protecting communities against fascism. I conclude by outlining what might be the central tenets of public pedagogy against fascism.

Reality

Global and US capitalism 2018

In the first section of chapter 3 of this book, I discussed three and a half decades of neoliberal capitalism in the US, including the global economic crisis of 2008, and resultant disillusionment with and alienation from mainstream politics and politicians that paved the way for the triumph of Trump and the consolidation of the alt-right. In the first part of this this chapter, I address the reality of global and US capitalism in 2018.

Inequality

Inequality.org (2018) provides the following figures for the state of capitalism worldwide and in the US:

- 70.1% of the world's adults own under $10,000 in wealth, just 3% of total global wealth.
- The world's wealthiest individuals, those owning more than $100,000 in assets, total only 8.6% of the global population, but own 85.6% of global wealth.
- Individuals worth more than £30 million own 12.8% of total global wealth.
- The world's 10 richest billionaires own $505 billion in combined wealth, a sum greater than the total goods and services most nations produce on an annual basis.
- 43% of the world's millionaires reside in the US.
- Wealth disparity in the US is running twice as wide – and more – as wealth gaps in the rest of the industrial world.
- The top 1 percent in the United States hold an average $15 million in wealth, a total only comparable to the prosperous microstate of Luxembourg; no other nation's top 1 percent own even half of the wealth the top 1 percent's in the United States and Luxembourg hold.
- The US dominates the global population of high net worth individuals, with over 4.3 million owning at least £1 million in financial assets (not including their primary residence or consumer goods).
- The US is home to more than twice as many adults with at least $50 million in assets as the next five nations with the most super-rich combined.
- The US has more wealth than any other nation, but top-heavy distribution leaves typical American adults with far less wealth than their counterparts in other industrial nations.

(Inequality.org, 2018)

In addition, summarizing an Oxfam report (Oxfam, 2018), *USA Today* reporter Kim Hjelmgaard (2018) points out that four out of every five dollars of wealth generated in 2017 ended up in the pockets of the world's richest 1%, while the poorest half of the world got nothing. Meanwhile, a new billionaire is created every other day; the three richest Americans have the same amount of wealth as the poorest half of the US population; and the number of billionaires worldwide total 2,043, of which nine out of ten are male. Collectively, their fortunes increased by $762 billion in 2017 and the poorest half of humanity saw no increase. Finally, the world's richest 1% continue to own more wealth than the rest of the global population combined (cited in Hjelmgaard, 2018). A projection produced by the UK House of Commons library suggests that if trends since the 2008 financial crash continue, by 2030 the top 1% will own nearly two-thirds of all wealth (cited in Savage, 2018). According to the World Income Inequality Database, the US has the highest Gini rate (measuring inequality) of all Western countries (Alston, 2017).

Poverty

As far as poverty is concerned, in one of the richest countries in the world, the official poverty rate is nearly 13%, that is to say over 40 million Americans (Center for Poverty Research, University of California, Davis, 2017). According to research from the National Center for Children in Poverty (NCCP) at Columbia University's Mailman School of Public Health, children make up around a quarter of the US population, but represent more than a third of the nation's poorest residents. Some 41 percent (29.8 million) of America's children were living on the brink of poverty in 2016 – including more than 5 million infants and toddlers under age three (Columbia University, 2018).

United Nations Special Rapporteur on extreme poverty and human rights Philip Alston spent two weeks in December 2017 visiting the US to look at whether the persistence of extreme poverty there undermines the enjoyment of human rights by its citizens. In his travels through California, Alabama, Georgia, Puerto Rico, West Virginia, and Washington, D.C., Alston spoke with 'dozens of experts and civil society groups, met with senior state and federal government officials and talked with many people who are homeless or living in deep poverty' (Alston, 2017). The 'dramatic cuts in welfare, foreshadowed by [Trump] and Speaker Ryan', he explains, 'already beginning to be implemented by the administration, will essentially shred crucial dimensions of a safety net that is already full of holes'. It is 'against this background that [his] report is presented' (Alston, 2017). Alston heard how 'thousands of poor people get minor infraction notices', which, he notes, 'seem to be intentionally designed to quickly explode into unpayable debt, incarceration, and the replenishment of municipal coffers'. In addition, he 'saw people who had lost all of their teeth because adult dental care is not covered by the vast majority of programs available to the very poor' and 'met with people in the South of Puerto Rico living next to a mountain of completely unprotected coal ash which rains down upon them bringing illness, disability and death'. In today's United States, 'contrasts between private wealth and public squalor abound' (Alston, 2017). He sums up:

> the United States is alone among developed countries in insisting that while human rights are of fundamental importance, they do not include rights that guard against dying of hunger, dying from a lack of access to affordable healthcare, or growing up in a context of total deprivation.
>
> (Alston, 2017)

Public pedagogy from 'some politicians and media' caricature 'narratives about the purported innate differences between rich and poor'. The rich 'are industrious, entrepreneurial, patriotic, and the drivers of economic success', while the poor 'are wasters, losers, and scammers'. 'As a result', Alston goes on, 'money spent on welfare is money down the drain'. 'To complete the picture', he concludes, 'we are also told that the poor who want to make it in America can easily do so: they really can achieve the American dream if only they work hard enough' (Alston, 2017). The reality that Alston has seen 'is very different'. Many of the 'wealthiest citizens do not pay taxes at the rates that others do, hoard much of their wealth off-shore, and often make their profits purely from speculation rather than contributing to the overall wealth of the American community' (Alston, 2017).

Meanwhile, racist stereotypes 'are usually not far beneath the surface', with the poor 'overwhelmingly assumed to be people of color, whether African Americans or Hispanic "immigrants"'. Some politicians and political appointees, Alston spoke to, are 'completely sold on the narrative of [welfare recipients] sitting on comfortable sofas, watching color TVs, while surfing on their smart phones, all paid for by welfare' (Alston, 2017). 'The face of poverty in America', he points out, 'is not only Black, or Hispanic, but also White, Asian, and many other colors' (Alston, 2017). 'The American Dream', in reality 'is rapidly becoming the American Illusion . . . since the US now has the lowest rate of social mobility of any of the rich countries' (Alston, 2017).

With respect to indigenous peoples, chiefs, and representatives 'from both recognized and non-recognized tribes' presented Alston 'with evidence of widespread extreme poverty in indigenous communities in the USA', calling for 'federal recognition as an essential first step to address poverty, indicating that without it their way of life is criminalised, they are disempowered, and their culture is destroyed', 'all of which perpetuate poverty, poor health, and shockingly high suicide rates' (Alston, 2017). 'Living conditions in Pine Ridge, Lakota', for example, 'were described as comparable to Haiti, with annual incomes of less than $12 000 and infant mortality rates three times higher than the national rate'. There, nine lives had been lost to suicide in the last three months, including, he stresses, one six year old. 'Nevertheless, federally funded programmes aimed at suicide prevention have been de-funded' (Alston, 2017).

Poverty is also gendered, with women shouldering 'a particularly high burden as a result of living in poverty'. Women are, for example, 'more exposed to violence, more vulnerable to sexual harassment, discriminated against in the labor market' (Alston, 2017). Alston cites Luke Shaefer and Kathryn Edin's (2018, 24) conclusion that the number of children in single-mother households living in extreme poverty for an entire year has ballooned from fewer than 100,000 in 1995 to 895,000 in 2011 and 704,000 in 2012. Perhaps, 'the least recognized harm', he concludes, 'is that austerity policies that shrink the services provided by the state inevitably mean that the resulting burden is imposed instead upon the primary caregivers within families, who are overwhelmingly women'. 'Male-dominated legislatures', he argues, 'rarely pay any heed to this consequence of the welfare cutbacks they impose'. (Alston, 2017).

Referring to racism experienced by African Americans, Alston describes it as 'a constant dimension' and regrets 'that in a report that seeks to cover so much ground there is not room to delve much more deeply into the phenomenon'. 'Racial disparities', he notes, 'already great, are being entrenched and exacerbated in many contexts' (Alston, 2017). He gives the example of Alabama, where he 'saw various houses in rural areas that were surrounded by cesspools of sewage that flowed out of broken or non-existent septic systems'. 'The State Health Department', he points out, 'had no idea of how many households exist in these conditions, despite the grave health consequences', nor, he goes on, 'did they have any plan to find out, or devise a plan to do something about it':

> since the great majority of White folks live in the cities, which are well served by government built and maintained sewerage systems, and most of the rural folks in areas like Lowndes County, are Black, the problem doesn't appear on the political or governmental radar screen.
>
> (Alston, 2017)

'The same applies to persons with disabilities', Alston (2017) points out:

> In the rush to claim that many beneficiaries are scamming the system, it is often asserted, albeit with little evidence, that large numbers of those receiving disability allowances are undeserving. When I probed the very high rates of persons with disabilities in West Virginia, government officials explained that most recipients had attained low levels of education, worked in demanding manual labor jobs, and were often exposed to risks that employers were not required to guard against.

Finally, with respect to environmental sustainability, it is not just Alabama that has issues with sewerage. Both there and in West Virginia, Alston was informed of the high proportion of the population that was not being served by public sewerage and water supply services. 'Contrary to the assumption in most countries that such services should be extended systematically and eventually comprehensively to all areas by the government', he concludes, 'in neither state was I able to obtain figures as to the magnitude of the challenge or details of any government plans to address the issues in the future' (Alston, 2017).

The overall picture, then, from Alston's visit is of an administration at best disinterested in the plight of poor Americans. The 2015 Nobel laureate in economics Angus Deaton has compared poverty in the US with the developing world. According to the World Bank, he informs us, 769 million people lived on less than $1.90 a day in 2013, the world's very poorest. Of these, 3.2 million live in the United States (Deaton, 2018). Deaton points out that the figures miss a very important fact. The World Bank adjusts its poverty estimates for differences in prices in different countries, but ignores differences in needs. An Indian villager, for example, 'spends little or nothing on housing, heat or child care, and a poor agricultural laborer in the tropics can get by with little clothing or transportation' (Deaton, 2018). Even in the United States, it is no accident that there are more homeless people sleeping on the streets, in cars or other makeshift situations in the warmer climate of Los Angeles (75% of its homeless) than in New York (4%) (Elliott, 2018, cited in Deaton, 2018). When we compare absolute poverty in the United States with absolute poverty in India, or other poor countries, we should be using $4 (estimate by Oxford economist Robert Allen) in the United States and $1.90 in India' (Deaton, 2018).

Once we do this, Deaton concludes, 'there are 5.3 million Americans who are absolutely poor by global standards', a small number compared with India, for example, but more than in Sierra Leone (3.2 million) or Nepal (2.5 million), about the same as in Senegal (5.3 million) and only one-third less than in Angola (7.4 million) (Deaton, 2018). Deaton (2018) concludes: 'There are millions of Americans whose suffering, through material poverty and poor health, is as bad or worse than people in Africa or Asia'.

In June, 2018, the US withdrew from the United Nations Human Rights Council, calling it a 'cesspool of political bias' (Borger, 2018).

Trump against the US working class

As Karla Walter and Alex Rowell (2018) write, on the campaign trail Donald Trump cast himself as the savior of the working class, 'willing to buck both the Republican and Democratic establishment in order to stand up for working people'. This has not happened in practice. In order to demonstrate this, I will look first at that proposed tax bill, much heralded and hyped by Trump and by corporate America; then at workers' rights and equal opportunities in the workplace.

The tax bill: tilting the tax system further against the workers

As Lance Selfa (2018a), author of *U.S. Politics in an Age of Uncertainty* (Selfa, 2018b) writes of Trump, 'With his characteristic know-nothing braggadocio', he 'congratulated himself for signing a massive corporate tax cut bill' in December, 2017:

> All of this, everything in here, is really tremendous things for business, for people, for the middle class, for workers. I consider this very much a bill for the middle class and a bill for jobs.
>
> (cited in Selfa, 2018a)

Later, Selfa (2018a) points out, Trump noted that 'Corporations are literally going wild'. While almost every independent analyst would concur with this later comment, it is not so true of the middle class and the workers.

Selfa (2018a) explains that there are two major points to note. First, under the tax law, all of the cuts in corporate taxes are permanent, while cuts for individuals expire in 2025. This means that, according to the Tax Policy Center (2017a), 53 percent of Americans will be paying *more* in taxes in 2027 than they did in 2017, with the bulk of the tax increases concentrated on the *bottom 40 percent* of US households.

Second, even if most households see some tax cuts in the next few years, the biggest reductions by far will go to those in the top 5 percent of income distribution (Selfa, 2018), with the top 1 percent capturing more than 80% of the tax cuts (Tax Policy Center, 2017b). At the same time, in 2019, foreign investors will receive $5 billion more than every working- and middle-class American household in the states that voted for President Trump, combined (Rowell and Hanion, 2017).

Selfa (2018a) reminds readers of Trump's inaugural speech in which he promised that, 'Every decision on . . . taxes . . . will be made to benefit American workers and American families'. Selfa's (2018a) response is:

> With an administration and Congress whose one major legislative achievement for the entire year was a bill that further shifts the tax burden from corporations to ordinary Americans, it's easy to see that Trump's 'populism' was as much a con as Trump University.[1]

William Barber and Liz Theoharis (2017), co-chairs of the Poor People's Campaign (discussed later in this chapter), have described the tax bill as 'an act of gross violence against America's poor to serve the country's richest and most powerful', that has been 'a plan of white nationalists . . . throughout history to divide and conquer people at the bottom'. As they point out, the 'tax cut' will add $1.4 trillion to the national debt, 'setting the stage for deeper cuts to public goods'. In the short term, they suggest, we could see cuts to Medicare and Medicaid; and in the long term, 'massive cuts to social security and other programs that sustain the poor, the elderly, and the most vulnerable'. They conclude, 'our elected leaders would rather fight a war on the poor than a war on poverty' (Barber and Theoharis, 2017). More recently, Barber (cited in Smith, 2018b) has noted that the three trillion dollars transfer of wealth as a result of the 'tax reform' is the largest 'since the wealth that was transferred from slaves to the slave owners' aristocracy' (estimated at between $5.9 and $14.2 trillion – Craemer, 2015, cited in Main, 2015). Alston (2017) describes Trump's 'tax reform package' as 'America's bid to become the most unequal society in the world'.

Attacking workers' rights in the workplace

Karla Walter, director of the American Worker Project at the Center for American Progress (CAP) Action Fund, and Alex Rowell, research associate with the American Worker Project at CAP Action (2018), have provided full details of a number of Trump's betrayals of the US working class (Walter and Rowell, 2018) in addition to his signing into law a tax bill that tilts the tax system further against the workers. These include:

- attacks on the unions such as making it easier for companies to hire anti-union consultants (rescinding an Obama-era protection);
- urging the Supreme Court to undermine public sector unions;
- making it harder for workers to bargain with the companies that influence their working conditions;
- beginning to roll back rules that reduced unnecessary delays in the union election process and made it easier for unions to contact eligible voters;
- limiting workers' ability to decide with whom they want to form a union by making it easier for employers to manipulate bargaining units by adding in workers they feel would oppose the union.

Other anti-worker measures include undermining career training programs (by re-writing another Obama-era protection), slashing funding for job training and lowering the quality and pay of apprenticeship programs. In addition, Obama-era guidance was withdrawn that strengthened wage theft enforcement by ensuring that companies did not illegally misclassify their workers as independent contractors, and that when workers were cheated out of wages, 'joint employment' standards were enforced against the companies with the power to ensure legal compliance. In a separate rule change, employers were given full control over the tips that their workers receive (thus reversing protections instituted by the Obama administration). And another Obama-era protection, extending overtime rights to 4.2 million people, was derailed by the Trump administration. Further measures include limiting workers' rights to sue; threats to cut programs to aid struggling coal miners and their communities (a scheme developed and implemented by the Obama administration); and letting off the hook companies with long records of violating workplace laws by continuing to give them federal contracts, thereby repealing yet another Obama protection (Walter and Rowell, 2018).

With respect to Health and Safety, there are proposals to weaken safety protections for offshore drilling workers, eliminating a requirement for third-party inspections of safety equipment; to make key safeguards optional; to allow for industry self-policing; and to delay and weaken a mine inspection rule requiring mine operators to inspect their mines daily before allowing workers to go inside. Furthermore, it is being proposed that miners can be sent in before inspections are finished (Walter and Rowell, 2018).

As far as toxic materials are concerned, the Trump administration announced that it would roll back safety rules protecting workers from beryllium, a toxic metal that causes lung cancer and other deadly diseases. Although the administration is leaving in place Obama-era beryllium protections for workers in defense and aerospace industries, it would rescind requirements for medical exams, exposure monitoring, and other protections for construction and shipyard workers (Walter and Rowell, 2018). Another measure is delaying critical updates to the Environmental Protection Agency (EPA)'s Risk Management Program (RMP) until February 2019. The updates require facilities using and storing potentially toxic or dangerous chemicals to mitigate risks, thereby helping workers and local emergency responders plan for potentially catastrophic chemical accidents. The Obama administration had directed the EPA to improve safety requirements after a 2013 explosion killed 15 people. Walter and Rowell (2018) also document delays to the implementation of safety regulations; letting lawbreakers off the hook for violating them (reducing the amount of time companies are required to keep accurate records of worker injuries in dangerous industries from five years to six months); and reversing an earlier decision to ban chlorpyrifos – an agricultural pesticide – even after agency scientists completed an extensive risk assessment that concluded that it could damage the neurological development of children and cause acute symptoms in those exposed to even small amounts (Walter and Rowell, 2018).

Despite repeated defeated attempts to repeal the Affordable Care Act of 2010 (Obamacare), Trump used his administrative power to sign an executive order threatening working families' access to healthcare and leading to health insurance premiums spiking dramatically in many states, thus undermining many Americans' ability to purchase affordable health insurance. Walter and Rowell (2018) record one more attack on the American working class as a whole: proposing taking food off the tables of struggling workers and their families by making deep cuts to nutrition assistance, including the Supplemental Nutrition Assistance Program (SNAP), formerly known as food stamps.

Undermining equal opportunities in the workplace

Unsurprisingly, given Trump's racism, sexism, misogyny, and general disdain for equal opportunities issues (see chapters 1 and 2 of this book), there have also been measures to undermine equal opportunities at work. One such action was the Trump-appointed administrator's decision to allow companies to submit to the Equal Employment Opportunity Commission (EEOC) an older version of a yearly form with demographic information on their employees, rather than a newer one issued by the EEOC. The newer one requires summary pay data on employees, sorted by gender, 'race', and ethnicity across the ten job categories included on the form. This effectively makes it harder for enforcement agencies to combat gender and 'racial' pay disparities (Walter and Rowell, 2018).

We saw in chapter 1 of this book how Trump's policies affect people with disabilities, when his administration called twice for cuts to a program that delivers meals to disabled people, which one volunteer for the program described as a 'disaster'. We also saw how a disability activist described Trump's announcement in 2018 that states will be allowed to require Medicaid recipients to work in order to get health benefits as a move towards an America that does not provide a safety net for the most vulnerable.

With respect to LGBT Americans, we also saw in chapter 1 how Trump attempted unsuccessfully to ban transgender people from the military. In addition, under sweeping authority given to him by Trump, Attorney General Jeff Sessions, late in 2017, issued a direction that undercuts federal protection for LGBT people, telling agencies to do as much as possible to accommodate those who claim their religious freedoms are violated. A claim of a violation of religious freedom is now enough to override many anti-discrimination protections for LGBT people and others. (Guardian Staff, 2017).

In Trump's proposed budget for the fiscal year 2018 there is a plan to essentially eliminate the Office of Federal Contract Compliance Programs, which helps ensure that federal contractors do not discriminate against their workers on the basis of race, sex, sexual orientation, gender identity, religion, national origin, disability, or status as a protected veteran, thus weakening protections for the more than one in five Americans who work for a company that receives federal contracts (Walter and Rowell, 2018).

Attacking workers' retirement plans

Finally, there have been attacks on workers' retirement plans, delaying the enforcement of new protections that would require retirement advisers to act in the best interest of their clients for 60 days, without which advisers can recommend investments that are in their own best interests rather than their clients. Retirement savings plans have been shut down, repealing Obama-era guidance that helped cities and states set up retirement savings plans for workers without access to employer-provided plans and ending myRA ('my retirement account'), a public option for workers to start saving for retirement and other life goals through a safe, affordable, and portable *Roth* individual retirement account (where there is no income tax on withdrawals in retirement) (Walter and Rowell, 2018).

As director of lobby group, Good Jobs Nation, Joseph Geevarghese, put it, workers' rights have been systematically attacked in a way that will affect labor for decades to come (cited in Rushe, 2018). And there is more to come. According to Dominic Rushe (2018), there are 90 more pieces of legislation in the pipeline. These include the Outdoor Recreation Enhancement Act, which would block requirements that federal government contractors at national parks pay workers $10.10 an hour, overtime, and sick pay; and the Future Logging Careers Act, which will expand the use of child labor in the forestry industry so that 16- and 17-year-olds can work in logging under adult supervision. In addition, the Environmental Protection Agency (EPA) is considering a rollback of a 2015 rule that banned children under 18 from working with toxic pesticides (Rushe, 2018).

Above, I have outlined some to the Trump administration's anti-union measures. Rushe believes that 2018 could be a 'disaster' for unions, bringing 'financial calamity'. As he explains, the case *Janus v American Federation of State, County, and Municipal Employees* is financed in large part by the conservative Bradley Foundation. It argues that non-union members who are forced to pay an 'agency fee' to cover the expense of representing them in wage negotiations etc. should be exempted because they should not be forced to subsidize a union's political spending.

A similar case, *Friedrichs v California Teachers Association*, he goes on, ended in deadlock at the Supreme Court. Now that Trump has put conservative justice Neil Gorsush on the court, the unions are expecting to lose, with some preparing for losses of a third of their income (Rushe, 2018).

Under Obama, the National Labor Relations Board (NLRB), which oversees the rights of private sector workers to form unions, made franchised companies, like McDonald's, liable as 'joint employers' for unfair labor practices at businesses they effectively control. This rule, Rushe (2018) concludes, is being rolled back by the Trump administration.

As Walter and Rowell (2018) conclude, despite his pledge to support American workers:

> As president . . . Trump has not followed through on this promise. His administration is quietly using its executive and regulatory powers to roll back important protections for working people. And in every instance where Congress has passed a piece of anti-worker legislation, President Trump has signed the bill into law.

Trump's treatment of the US working class, therefore, stands in stark contrast to his pro-worker rhetoric, and does nothing to ease the glaring, rampant and increasing inequalities and poverty in today's USA. On the contrary, it exacerbates them. I now turn to forms of resistance to Trump, specifically anti-Trump protests, and to fascism, focusing on the role of Antifa in constraining the activities of the alt-right.

Resistance to Trump and to fascism

Anti-Trump protests

As Anthony Zurcher (2018) reminds us, 'Once upon a time there was an active, vocal resistance among conservatives to the prospect of Donald Trump's presidency' – not so by the start of 2018. In February of that year, speaking at the Conservative Political Action Conference, Trump's clearly intended objective was to drive home the point that he has governed as a true conservative, boating of tax cuts, right-wing judicial nominations, regulatory rollbacks and defense of religious liberty. According to straw poll of conference attendees, 93% approve of what Trump is doing, not too far from the 80% of Republicans across the US who continue to support him (Zurcher, 2018).

Outside the right-wing political mainstream, however, a different story is revealed. Wikipedia (ongoing)[2] have provided a useful timeline of anti-Trump protests, alongside significant events in Trump's ascendancy, from the announcement that he was standing for president right up to the present. It should be pointed out that the timeline also includes pro-Trump rallies and protests. The protests started on June 17, 2015, the day after Trump announced his candidacy, when the first documented protest at his first rally witnessed three protesters holding up signs. This was followed by another thirteen protests in 2015. From the beginning of the Republican primaries until Trump became the winner, there were a further sixteen protests (January to May 2016). There followed another nine protests until the official nomination (May to August 2016), after which there were seven up until his election victory. One protest involved a decision to publish one anti-Trump song per day for 30 days that was extended to 50 songs in 30 days.

After the victory announcement, large protests broke out on November 9 in Canada, the UK, France, Germany, Philippines, Australia, Israel, and elsewhere, with some continuing for several days. In the US on the same day, there were protests in some twenty US cities, and at various universities, colleges, and high schools. The following day, protests occurred in 14 cities, and on November 11, 2016, in twenty-one cities and at fourteen universities. Similar protests continued up until November 15. On November 16, students around the country walked out of classes, declaring their institutions 'sanctuary campuses' from Trump's planned immigration policy, while around 350 Harvard faculty signed a letter urging the administration to denounce hate speech. Further protests occurred over the next few days, and on November 19 three separate protests converged on the heavily secured area surrounding Trump Tower, and international protests occurred in Toronto, Melbourne, and Paris. The following day, a 69-year-old man wearing a US Marine uniform set himself on fire after proclaiming the need to protest Trump's election. He was hospitalized in stable condition. On the same day, in the middle of their new song, 'Bang Band', the group Green Day chanted, 'No Trump, no KKK, no fascist USA!' Protests continued throughout November, December, and January 2017, with multiple protests taking place on the day of Trump's inauguration, January 20.

The following day, a series of political rallies, known as Women's Marches, took place in over twenty countries around the world. In the US, the women's marches were one of, if not the largest, protests in American history, drawing crowds of over 3 million nationwide (Morris, 2018).The protests continued throughout 2017 and into 2018, with nearly 3 million attending the second women's march in March 2018 (Spillar, 2018).

In the same month, following an incident when 17 people were gunned down in a high school in Parkland, Florida, well over 1 million people participated in more than 800 demonstrations in all 50 states and 390 of the country's 435 congressional districts in March for Our Lives demonstrations (London, 2018d). As Eric London (2018d) argues, the demonstrations, coming in the midst of a wave of strikes and protests among teachers, 'mark a significant development in the growth of social opposition in the United States', with the 'large turnout and prominent role of high school students . . . a powerful sign of political radicalization among a generation of youth whose lives have been overshadowed by war, state repression, and rampant social alienation and dysfunctionality produced by the extreme growth of social inequality' (see the beginning of this chapter). One Latinx student, Edna Chavez, told the march in Los Angeles that addressing mass shootings required getting to the 'root causes' of social violence, which meant 'changing the conditions that foster violence', including joblessness, inequality, and a deteriorating public school system (cited in London, 2018d).

Protests continue as this book goes to press.

Antifa against the alt-right

Antifa has been very successful since Trump's election in challenging the alt-right, and in curtailing its ability to promote its fascist views both with respect to conventional institutional pedagogy and by public pedagogy. The first relates to the extreme difficulty for the alt-right to gain successful access to college and university campuses (this also, of course, curtails public pedagogy since political conflict that occurs on campuses is broadcast throughout the US, and indeed the rest of the world via conventional and social media). The second refers to restrictions on alt-right public pedagogy, given the loss of access to social media sites. The alt-right is also fractured and swamped with infighting, as well as losing members through naming and shaming, and losing support on account of its aggressive behavior. In a video uploaded in March 2018, focusing on the impossibility of his making college tours, Spencer (2018) admits that the alt-right is losing the ability to appear in public days after violent clashes between alt-right supporters and 500 counter-protestors at Michigan State University (Hughes, 2018). Spencer stresses that this is because of the success of Antifa in intimidating his supporters and shouting down his lectures:

> When they become violent clashes and pitched battles, they aren't fun. I really hate to say this, and I definitely hesitate to say this. Antifa is winning to the extent that they're willing to go further than anyone else, in the sense that they will do things in terms of just violence, intimidating, and general nastiness.
>
> (cited in Lennard, 2018)

It is ironic to say the least that a neo-Nazi should be complaining about 'general nastiness'!

Spencer also claims: 'I don't inspire any kind of violence . . . Until the situation changes, we are up a creek without a paddle' (cited in Hughes, 2018). The Southern Poverty Law Center responded that it was 'preposterous' that Spencer was surprised by the vehement opposition he faces. As SPLC's spokesperson, Ryan Lenz remarked, 'He said he wanted to go into the belly of the beast [in Spencer's own words, 'academic, Marxist-controlled territory']. And when the violence presented itself . . . Spencer chose to pick up on that and recraft the message' (cited in Hughes, 2018). Responding more generally to the policies of Spencer's claim that he does not inspire any kind of violence, it is, of course, inevitable that a white ethno-state could only be created by Hitler-like atrocities on a mass scale. As one Antifa activist noted on another occasion, 'Quite frankly, neo-Nazis believe that at some point they will have to commit horrific acts of violence in order to see their world view achieved, to murder non-white en masse' (cited in Thomas-Peter, 2018b).

Spencer ended his video by urging his supporters to be patient and keep the faith while he figures out what to do, and by re-iterating that he is missing the fun (Spencer, 2018). We have seen in this book how an extremely warped and dangerous sense of 'fun' permeates the alt-right.

Anti-fascist activists, Michael Hayden (2018) points out, agree with Spencer that the alt-right is 'up the creek', arguing that the recent failure of alt-right events in general is evidence of their success in opposing them. Hayden cites Mark Bray, an activist and academic, author of the book that was rushed into print after Trump's Charlottesville comments about very fine people on both sides, *Antifa, The Anti-Fascist Handbook*, as stating that the end of Trump's first year left him feeling 'optimistic' that white supremacists could no longer organize effectively in public. Bray argued that Charlottesville and the lackluster and aborted rallies that followed it showed that the alt-right cannot 'occupy a public space without it being a moment of crisis' (cited in Hayden, 2018), meaning that these events inevitably lead to arrests, backlash, and infighting. Bray, who toured the country for his book and spoke to thousands of people about antifascism, made the point that 'antifascism historically rises and falls in direct proportion to actions of the far-right', and believed that leftists would likely return to a different kind of activism as the threat of alt-right public marches subsides (Hayden, 2018). Kit O'Connell, another writer and a long-time anti-fascist organizer, argued at the end of 2017: 'They started out the year in a position of strength. Now, they can't go viral on Twitter or Facebook anymore. And, they can't mobilize in public without expecting to be massively opposed' (cited in Hayden, 2018).

It should be pointed out here that Antifa's public pedagogy of defense of anti-fascists and aggression towards fascists when it considers it necessary are not confined to the street. As one Portland Antifa member 'Lucy' told Sky reporter Hanna Thomas-Peter (2018b), much of their group's most important work happens away from the streets, often using sophisticated techniques to track down white supremacists online:

> I think they get much more scared when we know their names, when we know their addresses, where they work, that certainly makes them more afraid. When we release someone's place of work, our hope is to get them fired. Any second that a Nazi is spending looking for work, or

looking for housing if they've been evicted, is time they're not spending organising.

(cited in Thomas-Peter, 2018b)

Lucy's colleague 'Carter' adds:

> It's a very genuine threat, you know they're organising, they're emboldened, and they are committing murders. Dylann Roof, a neo-Nazi, murdered people in South Carolina . . . There have been cases in Portland of anti-fascists being attacked and neo-Nazis consistently murder people here and around the globe. These are real threats to our community, and the more we oppose them, the safer our communities are.

(cited in Thomas-Peter, 2018b)

As Thomas-Peter (2018b) explains, in Portland, Jeremy Christian has come to embody that threat. In May, 2017, he stabbed two men to death because they attempted to stop him shouting abuse at some schoolgirls. One of them, black American Destinee Mangum, who was traveling with an un-named Muslim friend, said they were told by Christian that they should go back to Saudi Arabia and that they should just kill themselves (Lion and Mortimer, 2017). Mangum told Thomas-Peter (2018b): 'He said . . . we shouldn't be here and we don't deserve to live. His eyes were kind of black almost and like I was just staring at him while he was talking and he was looking right back at me and that's when I was terrified' (cited in Thomas-Peter, 2018b).

As one Antifa supporter told Thomas-Peter (2018b): 'We can't give fascists an inch or they will take a mile, we've seen that before in Europe, they have to be quashed when they are small and by any means necessary'.

It is, of course, extremely good news for anti-fascists that Spencer is 'up the creek'. Michael Hayden (2018) provides other grounds for optimism, pointing out that, in addition to the calling off of rallies because of massive opposition by a diverse group of anti-fascists, and being purged from mainstream social media platforms:

- The alt-right is now fractured and swamped with infighting;
- The public naming and shaming of those who marched in Charlottesville has thinned its ranks;
- Its outright violent behavior has triggered an ongoing debate about the public face of the alt-right.

I argued in chapter 3 of this book that Charlottesville was a major moment for the alt-right. This is in the sense that the year 2017 will be remembered as the year fascism came back to the streets of America and the alt-right became known throughout the US, and indeed much of the world. It is ironic, therefore, that, if as Burley (2018) believes, it marked the beginnings of a decline. As he argues, alt-right 'leaders' had thought they had grown large enough in the wake of Trump and his unaligned supporters they could lead what was a mass movement on the streets of Charlottesville. In the event, according to Burley, they had to phone in hundreds of more traditional white nationalists (Burley, 2018). While these groups would have been sympathetic ideologically to alt-right, they would probably not at the time have considered themselves part of *the* alt-right.

The decline of the *street* presence, and accompanying public pedagogy, of the alt-right appears to be continuing. The several dozen activists who showed up outside the White House on August 13, 2018 to mark the one-year anniversary of Charlottesville – Unite the Right 2 – were overwhelmingly outnumbered by thousands of counter-protestors that included Antifa; socialists and communists; LGBT liberation groups; and politically minded D.C. citizens (Jenkins, 2018). The day before the planned event, Spencer had stated, 'I don't really see much potential for good things coming out of this. There's certainly a potential for danger. It will most likely will [sic] be a bit of a dud' (cited in Jenkins, 2018).

Public pedagogy against fascism

Hopefully, this book itself amounts to public pedagogy against fascism. I have considered some of the features of classical fascism leading up to and including World War 11. I have examined in some detail the fascistic Trump and the neo-Nazi alt-right, particularly the latter's concept of a white ethnostate, which, if allowed to happen could lead to another Holocaust. In this respect, Holocaust education, both institutional and via public pedagogy remains imperative. Public pedagogy against fascism must also, I would argue, include 'no platform' for fascists (not allowing fascist groups a joint platform with other political parties and/or interest groups); no access to the media; and against fascists' right to participate in mainstream political debate. These are my reasons:

- giving a platform to fascists makes them appear acceptable and respectable, whereas fascists operate by instilling fear and claiming 'no right to be here' for specific groups (e.g. Jews, Muslims, people of color, Gypsy Roma and Traveller communities, Lesbian, Gay, Bisexual, Transgender people, disabled people and so on)
- 'no right to be here' can only be brought about by terror, internment, deportation, and murder

- the right for fascists to have free speech is less important than the right of those on the receiving end not to be intimidated and abused verbally and physically: physical attack tends to follow fascist victories
- giving a platform to fascists should not be seen as part of the 'democratic process', because if in power, fascists' aim is to smash any form of democracy
- fascists want to destroy *literally*, if considered necessary and/or expedient, specific constituencies of humankind (see Cole, 2012, 71–73).[3]

One of the most common arguments against 'no platform' is the 'slippery slope': once you 'no platform' fascists, 'no platforming' progressive groups and/or constituencies of people progressives would want to defend will follow. As Bray (2017, 156) argues, when addressed historically, efforts to deny a platform for fascists did not emerge from individuals suddenly wanting to silence fascists because they 'disagreed' with them, but out of historical struggle, 'often waged in self-defense, of movements of leftists – Jews, people of color, Muslims, queer and trans people, and others, to make sure that fascists do not grow powerful enough to murder them'. Rather than buying into the liberal notion that all viewpoints are valid, from an antifascist perspective, it is not about 'a neutral line beyond which right-wing politics cannot cross'. 'For revolutionary socialist anti-fascists, the question to ask is, "Who will win the political struggle?"' (Bray, 2017, 156). I return to a discussion of revolutionary socialism in the next chapter.

Conclusion

In this chapter, I began by examining the reality of global and US capitalism in 2018, with respect to inequality and poverty. I went on to detail the ways in which the policies of Donald J. Trump, contrary to what he claims, are in actuality, anti-working class. Moving to resistance, I discussed opposition to Trump in the form of protests, and the successful challenge to and the undermining of the activities of the alt-right by Antifa. I concluded the chapter with a consideration of public pedagogy against fascism. The subject matter of the next and final chapter of the book is the need for a broad front against fascism and capitalism and for a public pedagogy for socialism.

Notes

1 In February, 2018, a federal appeals court upheld a $25m settlement against Trump over the now-defunct university program, meaning thousands who were

lured to attend his expensive but overblown real-estate seminars will finally get most of their money back (Walters, 2018).

2 I realize that it is not normal academic practice to cite Wikipedia, because of possible inaccuracies. However, in this case, it was the most comprehensive source I could find, and is merely a list of events, rather than an analysis. From now on, except where I draw on sources not cited in the Wikipedia article, I will depart from normal academic practice by not listing the nearly 500 references. Readers can, of course, access these themselves by logging in to Wikipedia (ongoing).

3 This is in stark contrast to revolutionary socialists who want to replace an economic and political system – capitalism – with socialism, perceived as, in essence, truly democratic, in the real sense of the word, that is, under the rule of the people, by and for workers and communities (see chapter 6 of this book).

6 'A broad front against fascism and capitalism'

Reform, revolution, and a public pedagogy for socialism

Introduction

What then is to be done? Having devoted my attention to Trump and the alt-right in the first five chapters of this book, I now move on to a new terrain. The subject matter of this final chapter of the book is a public pedagogy against capitalism and for socialism. I begin with a discussion of some socialistic movements that are prominent in the US, including Our Revolution; the Democratic Socialists of America; and the Poor People's Campaign. I move on to two women's movements crucial in the era of Trump and the alt-right, One Billion Rising and the Metoo Movements, and to Black Lives Matter and the ANSWER Coalition (**A**ct **N**ow to **S**top **W**ar and **E**nd **R**acism). I then consider two socialist groupings, Redneck Revolt and the International Socialist Organisation, and some socialist parties, including the Party for Socialism and Liberation, the People's Congress of Resistance, the Workers World Party, and the Socialist Equality Party. I conclude the chapter and the book with some suggestions as to what a United Socialist States of America might look like. Given the hegemony of (neoliberal) capitalism, this entails a discussion of whether such a system can become a reality in the US, and indeed elsewhere.

A public pedagogy for socialism

In the last chapter, I chronicled the apparent decline of the alt-right, based in part on an article by Shane Burley. In heralding this phenomenon, Burley (2018) stresses that he is *not* predicting the alt-right's 'irrelevance and failure'. Indeed, one possibility, he suggests, is that it may embrace a more 'open fascism' (Burley, 2018) (presumably Burley means in the sense of openly declaring itself 'fascist' as an organization – a number of those who self-describe as alt-right, as we have seen, already do). For socialists, anti-hate (directed at Trump and others) and anti-fascist public pedagogy including street action, though absolutely essential, are not enough. There is a need to go beyond resistance and to counter the root cause of the despair, racism, nascent fascism, and accompanying inequality outlined at the beginning of chapter 5, that characterizes America and the rest of the world in the early decades of the twenty-first century. That root cause is (neoliberal) capitalism.

Peter McLaren has written on the role of socialists in the US in the era of Trump, and serving as a counter to the arguably over-optimistic analyses by some cited in the 'alt-right and Antifa' section of chapter 5 of this book, of the decline of the alt-right (the likes of Spencer, as of fascists generally, are always around: Spencer, as we saw, is already 'figuring out what to do next'):

> these are some theoretical issues we need to address . . . . We need massive anti-fascist protests, a broad front that is well-coordinated, that refuses to allow ideologies of ethnic genocide to become part of the mainstream discourse. And we need to align these protests with anti-capitalists, socialists, and anti-racists, feminists, LGBTQ groups. Whether to use violence as a tactic, or strategy for that matter, must be contextually specific to the imminent threat posed by the fascists and neo-Nazis. In other words, more militant antifascists have in the past (Charlottesville for example) defended non-violent anti-fascist groups from violence of the neo-Nazis. . . . The mainstream press opposes antifa, as a marginalized, extremist group on the left. Chomsky and others, including some Trotskyists, oppose antifa as a gift to the right.[1] So there are lots of strategic questions here . . . . In sum, we need a broad anti-fascist, anti-imperialist, anti-racist and anti-capitalist united front.[2]

As I will insist at the end of this chapter, these struggles must be seen in the context of saving our planet from ecological disaster. As McLaren (2013, 84) has written elsewhere:

> Our mother earth is convulsing, choking on the filth, the dye, the pesticides, the toxins, the effulgent splendour of chemicals and the dread unleashed by the furnaces of human greed. Her death throes are imminent unless we decelerate the planetary ecological crisis.

Socialistic movements

In this first sub-section of the chapter, I outline some of the key socialistic groupings in the US today. I use the term 'socialistic' not 'socialist' for similar reasons I have used 'fascistic' rather than 'fascist' throughout the book, in this case 'socialistic', to indicate leaning towards socialism, and being open to socialist ideas. In addition, I employ 'socialistic' to the movements and groups generally advocating *reform* and *gradual* progress towards socialism, often via the current established 'democratic' process, rather than via revolution. I put 'democratic' in inverted commas because having the right to vote in capitalist 'democracies' about every 5 years does not really amount to a real democratic choice for peoples. This is exacerbated when the only likely winners are neoliberal capitalist parties. The aforementioned British socialist (see chapter 3, endnote 5) Russell Brand refers to this charade as 'duplicitous pseudo democracy' (cited in Maisuria, 2016, 92). While the political 'democratic' process is claimed falsely to be just that – 'democratic'– no such claims are possible for the authoritarian top-down economic structures in these capitalist societies. As we shall see, the democratization of the economy is the project of socialism, not capitalism.

Our Revolution

The mission of Our Revolution (undated), the movement around Independent Vermont Senator and former contender for the Democratic presidential nomination Bernie Sanders, is to 'reclaim democracy for the working people of our country' through a 'political revolution', 'supporting a new generation of progressive leaders' and 'empowering millions to fight for progressive change and elevating the political consciousness'. Its aim is 'to make our political and economic systems once again responsive to the needs of working families'. Sanders's influence should not be underestimated. As of the summer of 2018, he is keeping his options open about whether to run again for president in 2020.

Sanders is fully engaged in public pedagogy. First, he is drawing millions of viewers for events he streams live on Facebook, delivering a series of speeches designed to counter Trump and offer his own progressive alternative vision. Second, for the midterms, he is planning to 're-activate his "distributed organizing network" of supporters – the massive network of volunteers who made tens of millions of calls and texts for his presidential campaign – to help Democrats Sanders supports'. Third, since the 2016 election, he has also built a massive collection of Facebook videos, circumventing the mainstream political press while attracting massive audiences. His Facebook page has 7.5 million followers, his campaign page, another 5 million, and his 'Medicare for all'-focused videos had more than 100 million views in six months (Bradner, 2018). However, as Eric Bradner (2018) concludes, the biggest events are Sanders' livestreams. He drew 1.1 million *live* viewers for a 'Medicare for all' town hall in early 2018 and 2 million viewers in total. While Sanders is most comfortable talking about his bread-and-butter issues like Medicare for all, climate change, college affordability and income inequality, his public pedagogy also confronts Trump head-on:

> What Trump and his friends are trying to do is exploit old fracture lines in our society – racism, sexism, homophobia, Islamophobia, religious bigotry. In these dismal times, it is more important now than ever that we offer a vision to the American people – a vision of hope; a vision of what this nation can become.
>
> (cited in Bradner, 2018)

Our Revolution and Sanders may be thought of as socialistic rather than socialist, in that, although he (and Our Revolution) self-describe(s) as 'democratic socialist', Sanders' politics are first and foremost 'social democratic' rather than revolutionary socialist. As he once put it, 'When I talk about democratic socialist . . . I'm looking at countries like Denmark and Sweden' (Shilton, 2016), countries that are classic versions of social democracy (see Maisuria, 2018, chapter 2). As Jordan Shilton explains, 'These societies, so the argument goes, allegedly show what can be achieved if capitalism is humanised and its worst excesses controlled by state regulation, high taxes on the wealthy, and relatively generous social services and welfare provisions', and this is what Sanders had in mind. The reality, in many ways, can be viewed as very different (for an explanation, see Shilton, 2016; see also Maisuria, 2018). Moreover, although claiming to be part of the Democratic Socialists of America (DSA) tradition, a movement discussed in the next section, Sanders has never been a member of the DSA.

Democratic Socialists of America

In their own words, the DSA (2018):

> believe that both the economy and society should be run democratically to meet human needs, not to make profits for a few. We are a political and activist organization, not a party; through campus and community-based chapters DSA members use a variety of tactics, from legislative to direct action, to fight for reforms that empower working people.

Founded in 1982, the DSA had roughly 6,000 dues-paying members for the duration of its history. It now has around 47,000 card-carrying members (Mahdawi, 2018), and, according to Amien Essif (2018), is the largest socialist [I would say 'socialistic'] membership organization in the US since the Second World War. Considering itself a 'big tent', hence accentuating its *socialistic* credentials, its members range on the political spectrum from left-leaning Democrats to more revolutionary socialists.

There is the possibility that the DSA might become more revolutionary, since, as Christine Riddiough, a member of DSA's electoral committee, explains, the people in their 20s who now make up the bulk of its membership were motivated to join the organization by Sanders, from whom they 'heard the phrase "democratic socialist" probably for the first time in their lives'. 'They have turned to DSA probably just because of the name' and they're now motivated to take action at the state and local levels (cited in Heyward, 2017). To be specific, as this younger generation educates itself in various ways, including via public pedagogy as to the real meaning of socialism, there are sound reasons to presume that they might push the DSA in a more revolutionary direction.

Poor People's Campaign

The 'Poor People's Campaign: A National Call for Moral Revival' is a radical Christian campaign, its main title named after Martin Luther King Jr's movement of the 1960s, that although it refers not to left vs right but to right vs wrong, associates itself with the later-in-life socialistic politics of King (see Cole, 2011b, 82–83), rather than merely the King of 'I have a dream' (Smith, 2018b). The Poor People's Campaign is a form of liberation theology Baptist-style that preaches a public pedagogy of love rather than one of hate. As Oliver Laughland (2017) points out, in 2016, its aforementioned co-chair William Barber gave an electrifying speech at the Democratic National Convention, calling for 'moral defibrillators of our time' to 'shock this nation with the power of love'. As the Campaign itself explains, in what could be seen as a direct reference to Trump: 'We uphold the need to do a season of sustained moral direct action as a way to break through the tweets and shift the moral narrative' (Poor People's Campaign, undated). Laughland (2017) describes the power of Barber's speech making:

> The oration is infectious, Barber's typical brand of liberation theology fusing constitutional politics and biblical principles of love and mercy. It makes not just the hairs on your neck stand on end, but your whole body sway.

The Campaign's platform includes justice for all and is against 'systemic racism, poverty (the US has an abundance of resources to overcome it), and ecological devastation'; dismantling unjust criminalization systems that exploit poor communities and communities of color and the transformation of the 'war economy' into a 'peace economy'. The Campaign aims to:

> shift the distorted moral narrative often promoted by religious extremists in the nation from issues like prayer in school, abortion, and gun rights to one that is concerned with how our society treats the poor, those on the margins, the least of these, women, LGBTQIA folks, workers, immigrants, the disabled and the sick; equality and representation under the law; and the desire for peace, love and harmony within and among nations.
>
> (Poor People's Campaign, undated)

The movement, which is not from above but below, 'will build up the power of people and state-based movements to . . . transform the political, economic and moral structures of our society'. Consistent with King's beliefs, it embraces nonviolence (Poor People's Campaign, undated).

Women's movements

In patriarchal societies, women's movements are always crucial. They take on added significance, given the sexism, anti-feminism and misogyny displayed and enacted by both Trump and the alt-right, as detailed throughout this book, even more so because of the role and treatment of women and girls in traditional fascism, and that proposed and envisaged by the alt-right. In the first part of this chapter, I referred to the Women's Marches. Two Women's *Movements* of note are 'One Billion Rising (2018)' and the 'MeToo Movements'.

One Billion Rising

Based in New York and named, in a three-word epithet of public pedagogy, after the number of women who get raped or beaten during the course of their lifetime, 'One Billion Rising' is in fierce opposition to Trump and the alt-right, and is internationalist in reach. The theme of the campaign for 2018, 'One Billion Rising Revolution' is 'Solidarity', with the slogan, 'Rise! Resist! Unite!' As the organization puts it:

> We are coming into a time defined by a fierce escalation of fascist, imperialist, neo-liberal attacks on the lives of people around the world. And the most marginalized – working class, minority and women on the margins in every part of the globe – experience the impact and are forced to confront these attacks on their welfare and rights and homes.
>
> (One Billion Rising, 2018)

Exploring its wide and far-reaching brief, it goes on that in response to Trump's election, joining 'the emergence of other anti-women, anti-people leaders and governments around the world':

> we are seeing mass global rising of movements and deep and ongo-ing engagement creating a vigorous solidarity and dynamic energy to a rising resistance everywhere – for women's rights and gender rights, the protection and defense of indigenous lands and the rights of indig-enous peoples, against fascism and tyranny, discrimination and racism, environmental plunder and destruction, corporate greed, economic vio-lence, poverty, state brutality and repression, war and militarism. This year, OBR is set to escalate RISINGS against all forms of violence against women – including a rising resistance against the systems that cause other forms of violence: imperialism, fascism, racism, capital-ism and neo-liberalism – and will continue to highlight where all these issues interconnect.
>
> (One Billion Rising, 2018)

MeToo

In 2006, Tarana Burke founded the me too #MeToo movement ('me too', itself a brief sobriquet of public pedagogy) to help survivors of sexual vio-lence, particularly young women of color from low wealth communities, find pathways to healing. Using the idea of 'empowerment through empa-thy', the movement was ultimately created to ensure survivors know they are not alone in their journey (MeToo, undated). By bringing vital conversa-tions about sexual violence into the mainstream, MeToo helps de-stigmatize survivors by highlighting the breadth and impact sexual violence has on women. It is a movement of 'silence breakers' based on the premise that nearly 18 million women have reported a sexual assault since 1988 (metoomvmt.org). On being named *TIME* magazine's 'Person of the Year' in 2017, Burke stated: 'A movement of survivors has been named the Per-son of the Year at a time when the President jokes about sexual assault in graphic detail' (metoomvmt.org).

Anthony Dimaggio (2018) is correct in pointing out that there is 'no ques-tion that the #MeToo movement is succeeding in directing much needed public attention to the issue of gender oppression', and that it is a 'serious component of the larger anti-Trump political movement that speaks to the legitimate anxieties of women who have long been treated like second-class citizens'. He is also right in stating that one problem with *the coverage* of the movement is 'that it is highly episodic, focusing on individual high-profile cases of sexism, rather than thematic and spotlighting broader trends in sexual harassment and assault throughout society'.

On this point, Burke, who, in her own words, 'grew up in [a] low-income, working-class family in a housing project on the Bronx' (cited in Brockes, 2018) was worried because victims of sexual violence might be poorly served by the publicity. As she explains to New York-based feature writer for the *Guardian* Emma Brockes, her two decades of doing grinding, unglamorous, financially ruinous work, setting up programs to help victims of abuse, didn't tend to include sharing their status online (Brockes, 2018). As it turns out, Burke now thinks that the de-stigmatising effect of #MeToo amounts to a greater gain that the anticipated risks, and, as far as the accusation of 'overcorrection' is concerned, she has seen what the alternative – doing nothing – looks like (Brockes, 2018).

On the issue of collateral damage and some men being overly punished for minor transgressions, Burke responds: 'I hate that . . . But I tend to pivot away from that because people tend to blow that up and make it the main thing; "What if she's lying?!" OK. But it's, like, a 3% chance' (cited in Brockes, 2018). She also disagrees that sexual violence and sexual harassment are unrelated, since while the latter should not be conflated with rape, they are on the same spectrum. Finally, underlining the crucial role in MeToo of the use of language as public pedagogy, Burke notes how concepts like 'rape culture' communicate 'at the most basic level: it isn't your fault' (cited in Brockes, 2018).

Black Lives Matter

In 2013, three radical black organizers – Alicia Garza, Patrisse Cullors, and Opal Tometi – created, in their own words, 'a Black-centered political will and movement building project called #BlackLivesMatter', in response to the acquittal of Trayvon Martin's murderer, George Zimmerman (Black Lives Matter: Herstory, undated). It is now 'a member-led global network of more than 40 chapters', organizing and building 'local power to intervene in violence inflicted on Black communities by the state and vigilantes' (Black Lives Matter: Herstory, undated). Its principles include creating 'a culture where each person feels seen, heard, and supported'; and acknowledging, respecting, and celebrating differences and commonalities; (Black Lives Matter: What We Believe, undated). Although Black Lives Matter works 'vigorously for freedom and justice for Black people and, *by extension, all people*' (emphasis added), it is 'unapologetically Black in [its] positioning'. It is

> guided by the fact that all Black lives matter, regardless of actual or perceived sexual identity, gender identity, gender expression, economic status, ability, disability, religious beliefs or disbeliefs, immigration status, or location.
>
> (Black Lives Matter: What We Believe, undated)

Black Lives Matter makes 'space for transgender brothers and sisters to participate and lead' and aims to 'uplift Black trans folk, especially Black trans women who continue to be disproportionately impacted by trans-antagonistic violence'. In addition, it builds a space that 'affirms Black women and is free from sexism, misogyny, and environments in which men are centered' (Black Lives Matter: What We Believe, undated).

Black Lives Matter is family-friendly, intent on dismantling 'the patriarchal practice that requires mothers to work "double shifts" so that they can mother in private even as they participate in public justice work', thus disrupting 'the Western-prescribed nuclear family structure requirement by supporting each other as extended families and "villages" that collectively care for one another, especially our children, to the degree that mothers, parents, and children are comfortable' (Black Lives Matter: What We Believe, undated).

Black Lives Matter fosters 'a queer-affirming network', in order to free itself 'from the tight grip of heteronormative thinking', or 'the belief that all in the world are heterosexual (unless s/he or they disclose otherwise)'. Finally, its public pedagogy cultivates 'an intergenerational and communal network free from ageism', believing that 'all people, regardless of age, show up with the capacity to lead and learn' and embodies and practices 'justice, liberation, and peace in [its] engagements with one another' (Black Lives Matter: What We Believe, undated).

Underlining the fact that Black Lives Matter is not *just* about black people, but also motivated by wider considerations of equality, historian, author, and longtime activist Barbara Ransby stresses:

> While the concerns raised by the Black Lives Matter movement reflect the experiences of most black Americans, they also extend beyond these communities. It is imperative that all progressive and left forces pay careful and respectful attention to this growing movement and its bold confrontation with state power. Its message is, in part, that there can be no real economic justice without racial justice . . . To focus on the black poor is not to ignore others who also endure economic inequality . . . . In other words, any serious analysis of racial capitalism must recognize that to seek liberation for black people is also to destabilize inequality in the United States at large, and to create new possibilities for all who live here.
>
> (Ransby, 2015)

The ANSWER Coalition

The ANSWER Coalition (**A**ct **N**ow to **S**top **W**ar and **E**nd **R**acism) was founded three days after the 9/11 (September 11, 2001) attacks on the World

Trade Center, and initiated the massive anti-war movement opposing the US invasion of Iraq in the months prior to March 19, 2003. On January 18, 2003, 500,000 people packed the Mall in Washington, D.C., the largest anti-war protest since the end of the Vietnam War (ANSWER, undated). In its own words, a 'distinguishing feature of the organizing principles and work of the answer coalition, in contrast with the traditional U.S. peace movement [is] its uncompromising support in defense of the rights of the Palestinian people'. It is also 'actively fighting against the ongoing occupation of Afghanistan, the renewed assaults on Iraq and Syria, the drone attacks on Yemen, Pakistan and Somalia, among others' (ANSWER, undated). ANSWER is centrally involved in fighting racism, religious profiling, and police brutality; in supporting immigrant and workers' rights; and in promoting economic and social justice, locally and internationally. According to Derek Ford (his comments on this book), the ANSWER Coalition is probably the most active organization nationally, leading the protest that shut down Trump in Chicago while on the campaign trail, and organized the protest at his inauguration.

Socialist groupings

Redneck Revolt

Redneck Revolt was founded in 2016 as an armed anti-racist, anti-fascist community defense formation. Its public pedagogy is articulated on its website:

> We need real formulated responses for the upsurge in reactionary and racist violence. We need armed community defense programs in every community. We need to be ready to rapidly respond to the armed right wing threat that menaces our communities. We need to stop being reactionaries when it comes to the topic of armed defense. We are approaching truly dangerous times.
>
> (Redneck Revolt, undated, a)

Although it does not use the term 'socialist' in its organizing principles, socialism is clearly indicated in its agenda, one that includes a demand that their communities, for which they are organized for defense as an aboveground militant formation, are entitled 'to all the wealth that we as workers produce' (Redneck Revolt, undated, b; see also Watt, 2017 where Redneck Revolt's socialism is made more explicit, but where reference is also made to anarchism). Redneck Revolt is against the nation state and its forces that 'protect the bosses and the rich', for

'community power and community rights over the rights of any government body' and on the side of 'working class people of every country of
the world against our common enemy: the rich and powerful'. Redneck
Revolt 'will not allow arbitrary borders or boundaries to prevent us from
unifying with other working class people'. It is against capitalism, rec-
ognizing that 'we will always have more in common with other working
people of all races and backgrounds than we could have with any rich person regardless of whether they share our same color of skin'. It is against
the wars of the rich (Redneck Revolt, undated, b).

Redneck Revolt is against patriarchy, noting that 'women, femme, queer,
and trans folks are disproportionately deprived of their liberty and threatened with violence', with the 'struggle against patriarchy [as] central [as]
our struggle against capitalism and the nation-state'. These folks:

> have long been discouraged from gaining the skills needed to defend
> themselves from violence and oppression, and together we seek to
> ensure we are all empowered to defend our communities. True libera-
> tion includes the freedom to live authentically and safely, regardless of
> our gender or sexual identity (Redneck Revolt, undated, b).

Last but not least, Redneck Revolt believes in the need for revolution in
order for there to be 'a complete restructuring of society to provide for the
survival and liberty of all people':

> We will fight for the end of predatory exploitation of our communities,
> and the creation of a world where no one is without food, shelter, water,
> or any other means of survival. We believe in a future without tyranny,
> and the political and social control of a small segment of society over
> the rest of us. We believe that the working class can unite across racial
> and cultural backgrounds and find we are much stronger with diverse
> perspectives. We believe in liberty. We believe in equity. We believe in
> the self-determination of our own futures (Redneck Revolt, undated, b).

International Socialist Organisation (ISO)

In its own words, the 'ISO is building a socialist alternative in a world of
poverty, oppression and war'. It 'participates in many different struggles for
justice and liberation today, while working toward a future socialist society,
free of all exploitation and oppression, and built on the principles of solidarity and democracy' (International Socialist Organisation, 2018).

A longstanding organization, ISO has branches and members in about 40
US cities and connections to other socialists around the world. It organizes

'in the here and now against injustice and for reforms that will benefit the working class and oppressed'. It notes that 'these struggles are important in their own right, but they are also building blocks for a movement to achieve a socialist society' (International Socialist Organisation, 2018).

ISO is a Trotskyist organization, after Leon Trotsky's Marxist-Leninist belief in a vanguard party of the working class, favoring world socialist revolution, rather than Stalin's version of 'socialism in one country', in that case the USSR. Its public pedagogy involves socialist work on the streets and in the unions and it has an active website, 'International Socialist Organisation' that includes podcasts, analyses of US and world issues and Marxist and Trotskyist theory.

Socialist parties

Party for Socialism and Liberation

The Party for Socialism and Liberation (PSL), 'comprised of leaders and activists, workers and students, of all backgrounds' is organized in branches across the US, bringing together a 'new generation of revolutionaries alongside veterans of the people's movements with decades of experience' (Liberation, undated).

The PSL is 'deeply involved in a wide range of struggles, from local battles over affordable housing and racist police brutality, to the fight for a higher minimum wage and union rights, to the global issues of imperialist war and environmental destruction' (Liberation, undated).

PSL members are united in a belief that 'capitalism – the system in which all wealth and power is held by a tiny group of billionaires and their [capitalist] state – is the source of the main problems confronting humanity today'. Capitalism, the PSL argues, must be replaced by socialism, 'a system where poor and working people have power and the wealth of society is used in a planned and sustainable way to meet people's needs'. Its mission is to link the everyday struggles of oppressed and exploited people to the fight for a new world (Liberation, undated). Its public pedagogy includes 'militant journalism', videos, books, and magazines, as well as 'party statements' on US and world issues.

People's Congress of Resistance

On September 16 and 17, 2017, the People's Congress of Resistance movement was inaugurated with a mass convening at Howard University of grassroots organizers and frontline resistors with deep ties to the communities they organize. Over 700 delegates from 38 states and 160 towns and cities came to Washington, D.C. (People's Congress of Resistance, 2017), to discuss the People's Congress of Resistance manifesto 'Society for the Many: A Vision for Revolution' (*Manifesto* of the People's Congress of Resistance, undated a; (People's Congress of Resistance, 2017). As the Congress explains:

> The United States Congress does not represent the people who live and work in the United States. Given the threat posed by the Trump regime, the people must take matters into our own hands, together, and claim the power we already have.
>
> (People's Congress of Resistance, undated b)

It goes on, 'The People demand a new Congress, a fighting Congress of the working class of all racial and ethnic backgrounds, genders and ages', in order to 'create a Congress of communities under attack by the reactionary Trump agenda and fighting back against it'. This must be 'a Congress of the grassroots and the working class, of resisters, organizers, and activists, of everyone who recognizes we can no longer continue as we have'. 'Such a People's Congress', it concludes, 'will confront the Congress of the millionaires. It will galvanize the energy of the many groups resisting Trump', in order to show what real democracy looks like (People's Congress of Resistance, Call to Action).

Workers World Party

Founded in 1959, the Workers World Party has branches around the US. It is 'a revolutionary Marxist-Leninist party dedicated to organizing and fighting for a socialist revolution in the United States and around the world'. It is active in the Black Lives Matter movement and advocates disarming the police and other repressive state apparatuses (Workers World Party 2018). In addition, the Workers World Party supports the lesbian, gay, bisexual, transgender, and queer struggles, and the fight for the rights of people with disabilities and women. In its own words:

> Workers World Party, both in theory and in practice, has made important contributions to the liberation of women, on the job and through the movement for reproductive justice, and of lesbian, gay, bi, trans and queer people from all forms of patriarchal views and attitudes rooted in class society, beginning in the women's liberation movement in the 1970s and following the heroic 1969 Stonewall Rebellion in New York where LGBTQ youth, led by transwomen of color, rebelled against police repression.

Anti-imperialist and internationalist to its core, the Workers World Party argues that the struggle against the capitalist 1% is a global struggle, its goal is to 'build, expand, and unite the various progressive movements to a broader multinational, working class, global struggle', envisioning a world without the 1%, and the 'mass suffering it promotes and maintains' (What is WWP? 2018).

Socialist Equality Party and World Socialist Web Site (WSWS)

Last but not least is the Socialist Equality Party, a revolutionary socialist Trotskyist party, and its influential organ of public pedagogy, the World Socialist Web Site (WSWS) that provides very sophisticated analyses of world capitalism and the need for a socialist future, not just pertaining to the US, but worldwide. I have drawn from the WSWS extensively throughout this book. In terms of struggle, the WSWS tends to be dismissive of most other left groups, which it describes as 'pseudo left'. It also underestimates the importance of groups based on issues other than social class.

Conclusion

In this chapter, I have examined a number of movements, groupings, and parties for progressive economic, political, and social reform and revolution. Public pedagogy for socialism goes beyond the social justice agenda of progressive public pedagogy theory, as outlined in this book, in that it is about nothing less than the promotion of the transformation of society to a post-capitalist, and socialist future. There can be no blueprint for a United Socialist States of America, since:

> [u]nlike the utopian socialists, who drew up intricate blueprints of post-capitalist society (which they sometimes attempted to put into practice on a small scale) [see Cole, 2008, 15–27, for a discussion and Marxist critique] Marx and Engels never speculated on the detailed organization of a future socialist or communist society. The key task for them was building a movement to overthrow capitalism. If and when that movement won power, it would be up to the members of the new society to decide democratically how it was to be organized, in the concrete historical circumstances in which they found themselves.
>
> (Gasper, 2009)

Here, however, are some pre-requisites, based in part on preceding analysis and on the proposals of various groupings:

- the redistribution of wealth in as equal a manner as possible
- the democratization of the economy, so that it is owned, and controlled *democratically* in the true sense of the word (rule of the people) *by* and *for* workers and communities

- the production of goods and services for *need* and not for profit
- the basic necessities (free food, drink, housing, healthcare, education, and childcare for all) as a right
- full equality for all, regardless of gender, ethnicity, sexuality, disability, and age, irrespective of faith or no faith, and no discrimination on grounds of these identities or any other identity
- open borders for people and equal rights for immigrants; closed borders for profiteers and warmongerers
- no death penalty
- no imperialism, colonialism or militarism
- self-determination for Native Americans
- the need to address climate change seriously; end fracking, pipelines, and extractivism
- follow the lead of indigenous peoples in protecting water, land, and air.

It cannot be stressed enough that the last three bullet points self-evidently are a *pre-condition* for the building of socialism in the USA, and must be central in a public pedagogy for socialism and ecology. As climate change is playing out in real time throughout the world, as I write this in the summer of 2018, quite literally, we will have no world in which to create a socialist future unless we prioritize ecological issues. Indeed, some socialists have insisted that, instead of referring to 'socialism', we should use the term 'ecosocialism'. As Ian Angus (2013), editor of the journal, *Climate & Capitalism*, puts it:

> the environmental crisis we face today is not a simple extension of capitalism's centuries-old war with nature. In the last half of the 20th century, what Marx and Engels called the 'metabolic rift' [a rupture in the interaction between humanity and nature, emanating from capitalist production] became *qualitatively wider, qualitatively more serious . . .* [B]ecause the metabolic rift has become a global ecological abyss, *socialists today must be ecosocialists*.

The fight against environmental destruction, Angus goes on, 'is *central* to the fight against capitalism'. In the twenty-first century, 'fighting capitalist ecocide must be at the heart of our vision, our program and our activity' (Angus, 2013). He concludes:

> Capitalism has driven us to a crisis point in the relationship between humanity and the rest of nature – if business as usual continues, major ecological collapse isn't just possible but probable, and that will put civilization at risk. There is a giant death sentence hanging over much

of our world, and capitalism is the executioner . . . socialists must be ecosocialists, and humanity needs an ecosocialist revolution.

(Angus, 2013)

Ecosocialism becomes all the more urgent in the light of Trump's (willful) ecological ignorance (see the last section of chapter 1 of this book) which adversely affects not just the US, but the whole world.

All this begs the question, is (eco) socialism in the US is possible, or indeed anywhere else, given the hegemony of (neoliberal) capitalism? In order to attempt to answer that question, we need to turn to Marxism. As Glenn Rikowski puts it (in Rikowski and Ocampo Gonzalez, 2018, 9):

> Marxism does not just seek to explain oppression but starts out from the fact that we live in an oppressive society and attempts to understand the *fragility* of capital's existence and development. Marxism focuses on the *weaknesses* of capital, starting out from its dependency on labour and the labour-power of labourers in capitalist society.

Rikowski is referring to the fact that, without labor power, there is no surplus value and, therefore, no profit. Thus capitalism is dependent on labor power to exist. Marxists refer to this as the labor theory of value: the worker gets only a proportion of the value she or he creates (how much is dependent on historical and socio-economic factors, not least the extent to which workers are able to successfully demand higher wages) and the rest is appropriated, or hived off, by the capitalist. While the value of the raw materials and of the depreciating machinery is simply passed on to the commodity in production, labor power is a peculiar, indeed unique, commodity, in that it creates new value. 'The magical quality of labour- power's . . . value for . . . capital is therefore critical' (Rikowski, 2001, 11). 'Labour-power creates more value (profit) in its consumption than it possesses itself, and than it costs' (Marx, 1894 [1966], 351). Unlike, for example, the value of a given commodity, which can only be realized in the market as itself, labor creates a new value, a value greater than itself, a value that previously did not exist. It is for this reason that labor power is so important for the capitalist in the quest for capital accumulation, and why for Marxists, exploitation is an objective fact (see Cole, 2011b, 42–44 for further explanation and a numerical example of how this works; see also Maisuria, 2018). This capitalist dependency on the exploitation of workers – human beings with potential or actual class consciousness (of this exploitation) as well as the source of capitalists' profits – makes capitalism inherently both fragile and weak.

Following John Holloway (1994, 40), Rikowski (2006, 3) argues that Marxism is also a theory that articulates the contradictions of capitalist oppression, giving it 'a special relevance for any person or movement interested in a radical transformation of society'. It is by 'analysing [these] contradictions . . . that weak points in capital's mode of existence and functioning can be located' and 'can become the point of focus, critique and political action' thus facilitating 'the formation of political strategies of maximum effect' (Rikowski, 2006, 3).

The central contradiction in the development of capital is 'the project of expelling labour power from the capitalist labour process through technological innovation' (Rikowski, in Rikowski and Ocampo Gonzalez, 2018, 14). The ever-increasing technological drive for productivity, in order to undercut rivals by making commodities more cheaply, means more machines ('dead labour' – since labor produces them) and less labor power (the source of profit). Thus there is a tendency for the rate of profit (the ratio of profit to investment) to fall, meaning that booms get shorter and slumps, longer and longer and deeper and deeper. As Samir Hinks (2012) explains, because profit can only come from human labor, 'as more and more capitalists invest in the new machinery the average labour time required to produce each commodity falls. This is what makes the rate of profit fall, as the ratio of surplus value to investment falls across the whole system'. It is important to stress that this is only a *tendency* rather than a law. The solution for the capitalist is to attack workers' conditions, for example, by increasing hours without increasing pay, giving workers less breaks, keeping them under greater surveillance and by laying off workers on contracts and replacing them with workers on zero hours contracts at very low rates of pay or the legal minimum wage if there is one.

Large numbers of people in the US and many other parts of the world have had enough of (neoliberal) capitalist exploitation and oppression; and in establishment political parties and politicians in general. As Nancy Fraser (2017) argues, 'masses of people throughout the world [have] stopped believing in the reigning common sense that underpinned political domination for the last several decades', having 'lost confidence in the bona fides of the elites' and are looking for 'new ideologies, organizations, and leadership'.

As fragility, weakness, contradiction, and crisis intensifies, the need for of a life beyond actually existing capitalism also intensifies, and, if coupled with a global political crisis, workers look for alternatives. This takes us back to Trump and the alt-right. Monbiot (2016) argues that in the US, the backlash against neoliberalism elevated a businessman rather than a politician to the highest office who paradoxically is 'just the kind of man that

Hayek worshipped' (see chapter 3, pp. 45–46 of this book). With no coherent politics, Trump is not a classic neoliberal, but 'he is the perfect representation of Hayek's "independent"; the beneficiary of inherited wealth, unconstrained by common morality, whose gross predilections strike a new path that others may follow'. That new path has spawned the neo-Nazi alt-right, whose public pedagogy, though hotly and successfully contested, has made dangerous inroads into the fabric of society in the United States; hence the urgent need for socialists to articulate in every way possible, including public pedagogy, the exploitative nature of capitalism as outlined above, and the essential features of a socialism of and for the twenty-first century.

Prominent Italian neo-Marxist writer and politician Antonio Gramsci (1891–1937) recognized that 'the educational relationship should not be restricted to the field of the strictly "scholastic,"' and that pedagogy is also public, since '[t]his form of relationship exists throughout society as a whole and for every individual relative to other individuals' (1971, 350):

> It exists between intellectual and non-intellectual sections of the population, between the rulers and the ruled, *élites* and their followers, leaders . . . and led . . . Every relationship of 'hegemony' is necessarily an educational relationship.
>
> (Gramsci, 1971, 350)

Bearing this in mind, what does this mean for the (public) pedagogy of progressives in general? They 'would do well', as Henry Giroux (2017) argues 'to take account of the profound educational transformations taking place among a variety of cultural apparatuses, which are really teaching machines, and in doing so reclaim pedagogy as a central category of politics itself'. What can Marxist theory tell us? In the era of Trump and the alt-right, as alienation intensifies, it also brings hope. In David Harvey's (2018) words:

> I can assert with some certitude . . . that the production of universal alienation [laid out by Marx] . . . is strongly linked to the progress of real subsumption of not only labour processes but many aspects of daily life under the power of capital in its various forms. It is out of the morass of these universal alienations that anti-capitalist movements, as opposed to nihilistic forms of protest and fascistic accommodations, must arise.

As this book goes to press (the summer of 2018), for the first time in Gallup's measurement over the past decade, Democrats or Democratic-leaning voters have a more positive image of socialism (57%) than they do of capitalism (47%). At the same time, fewer than half of young Americans as a whole (aged 18 to 19) view capitalism positively (45%), with 51% being positive about socialism (Newport, 2018).

Notes

1 Spencer's (2018) video offers a sharp rebuttal to what Natasha Lennard (2018) describes as 'the glut of claims that antifa practices serve as a gift to the far right'.
2 Peter McLaren, from comments on an earlier draft of this book.

References

Alexa. 2018. 'Top Sites in United States'. www.alexa.com/topsites/countries/US

Alston, Philip. 2017. 'Statement on Visit to the USA, By Professor Philip Alston, United Nations Special Rapporteur on Extreme Poverty and Human Rights'. Geneva: Office of the United Nations High Commissioner for Human Rights (OHCHR). www.ohchr.org/EN/NewsEvents/Pages/DisplayNews.aspx?NewsID= 22533&LangID=E

Anglin, Andrew. 2016. 'A Normie's Guide to the Alt-Right'. *Daily Stormer*, August 31. https://dailystormer.red/a-normies-guide-to-the-alt-right/

Angus, Ian. 2013. 'Why We Need an Ecosocialist Revolution'. *Climate and Capitalism*, July 2. http://climateandcapitalism.com/2013/07/02/why-we-need-an-ecosocialist-revolution-2/

ANSWER. undated. www.answercoalition.org/

The Associated Press. 2018. www.latimes.com/sns-bc-us-trump-immigration-quotes-20180112-story.html

The Atlantic. 2016. 'Hail Trump!: Richard Spencer Speech Excerpts November 21'. https://int.search.myway.com/search/video.jhtml?n=78489219&p2=%5ECP6% 5Exdm259%5ETTAB02%5Egb&pg=video&pn=1&ptb=D63A1AF6-6331-4931-8AAC-94838A9B6676&qs=&searchfor=hail+trump%2C+hail+our+people %2C+hail+victory&si=37&ss=sub&st=tab&tpr=sbt&trs=wtt

Badiou, Alain. 2016. 'Alain Badiou: Reflections on the Recent Election'. *Verso Blogs*. www.versobooks.com/blogs/2940-alain-badiou-reflections-on-the-recent-election

Barber, William and Theoharis, Liz. 2017. 'The Republican Tax Bill Is Not Just Immoral. It Is an Act of Violence'. *The Guardian*, December 1. www.theguardian. com/commentisfree/2017/dec/01/republican-tax-bill-immoral-violence?CMP= Share_iOSApp_Other

Baynes, Chris. 2018. 'Donald Trump Claims His Greatest Assets Are His "Mental Stability and Being, Like, Really Smart"'. *The Independent*, January 6. www.independent. co.uk/news/world/americas/us-politics/donald-trump-really-smart-latest-twitter-greatest-assets-mental-stability-dementia-fire-and-fury-a8145326.html

BBC News. 2016. 'Reality Check: Who Voted for Donald Trump?'. *BBC News*, November 9. www.bbc.co.uk/news/election-us-2016-37922587

BBC News. 2018. 'Trump Calls for Deportations Without Judicial Process', June 24. https://bbc.co.uk/news/world-us-canada-44594652

Beal, Vangie. 2018. 'Internet Meme'. www.webopedia.com/TERM/I/internet_meme.html

Beijer, Carl. 'Fascism's Pincer'. *Jacobin.* www.jacobinmag.com/2017/08/climate-change-fascism-inequality-wealth-racism

Beishon, Judy. 2018. 'World Economy: Ten Years Since the Crash' Socialist World', March 1. http://socialistworld.net/index.php/theory-analysis/economy/31-world-economy/9664-world-economy-ten-years-since-the-crash

Berlet, Chip. 2015. '"Trumping" Democracy: Right-wing Populism, Fascism, and the Case for Action'. December 12. Somerville, MA: Political Research Associates. www.politicalresearch.org/2015/12/12/trumping-democracy-right-wing-populism-fascism-and-the-case-for-action/

Black Lives Matter. undated. 'Herstory'. https://blacklivesmatter.com/about/herstory/

Black Lives Matter What We Believe. undated. https://blacklivesmatter.com/about/what-we-believe/

Borchers, Callum. 2017. 'Meryl Streep Was Right. Donald Trump Did Mock a Disabled Reporter'. *The Washington Post*, January 9. www.washingtonpost.com/amphtml/news/the-fix/wp/2017/01/09/meryl-streep-was-right-donald-trump-did-mock-a-disabled-reporter/

Borger, Julian. 2018 . 'US Quits UN Human Rights Council – "A Cesspool of Political Bias"'. *The Guardian*, June 19. https://theguardian.com/world/2018/jun/19/us-quits-un-human-rights-council-cesspool-political-bias

Bosworth, Richard J. B. 2006. *Mussolini's Italy: Life Under the Fascist Dictatorship, 1915–1945*, Harmondsworth: Penguin.

Bradner, Eric. 2016. 'Alt-right Leader: "Hail Trump! Hail Our People! Hail Victory!"'. *CNN Politics*, November 22. https://edition.cnn.com/2016/11/21/politics/alt-right-gathering-donald-trump/index.html

Bradner, Eric. 2018. 'Bernie Sanders Is Showing How He'd Run Against Trump in 20'. *CNN Politics*, February 3. www.cnn.com/2018/02/03/politics/bernie-sanders-2020-trump/index.html

Bray, Mark. 2017. *Antifa: The Anti-Fascist Handbook*, Brooklyn, NY: Melville House.

Brockes, Emma. 2018. 'Me Too Founder Tarana Burke: "You Have to Use Your Privilege to Serve Other People"'. *The Guardian*, January 15. www.theguardian.com/world/2018/jan/15/me-too-founder-tarana-burke-women-sexual-assault

Broich, John. 2016 'Normalizing Fascists'. *The Conversation*, December 12. http://theconversation.com/normalizing-fascists-69613

Brühlmeier, A. 2010. *Head, Heart and Hand: Education in the Spirit of Pestalozzi*, Cambridge: Sophia Books.

Bullock, Allan and Trombley, Stephen (eds). 1999. 'Lebensraum'. In *The New Fontana Dictionary of Modern Thought*, New York, NY: HarperCollins.

Burley, Shane. 2018. 'As the "Alt-Right" Strays From Its Roots, Will It Turn to Open Fascism?'. *Truthout*, January 16. www.truth-out.org/news/item/43232-as-the-alt-right-strays-from-its-roots-will-it-turn-to-open-fascism

Capriccioso, Rob. 2017. 'Dems Say President Trump Is Racist in Calling Sen. Warren Pocahontas'. *Indian Country Today*, February 16. https://indiancountrymedia

network.com/news/politics/dems-say-president-trump-racist-calling-sen-warren-pocahontas/

Carrier, Peter. 2006. *Holocaust Monuments and National Memory Cultures in France and Germany Since 1989*, New York, NY: Berghahn Books.

Center for Poverty Research, University of California, Davis. 2017. 'What Is the Current Poverty Rate in the United States?', December 18. https://poverty.ucdavis.edu/faq/what-current-poverty-rate-united-states

Chalfant, Morgan. 2018. 'Ex-military Officials Sign on to Oppose Trump's Transgender Troops Ban'. *The Hill*, July 4. http://thehill.com/policy/defense/395513-former-military-officials-sign-on-to-oppose-trumps-transgender-troops-ban?amp

Chung, Alison and Culbertson, Alix. 2018. 'African Countries Demand President Trump Apology Over "shitholes" Slur'. http://news.sky.com/story/trump-in-excellent-health-after-physical-examination-says-doctor-11205380

CNN Politics. 2018. 'State of the Union 2018: Read the Full Transcript'. January 31. https://edition.cnn.com/2018/01/30/politics/2018-state-of-the-union-transcript/index.html

Cogan, James. 2018. 'Trump's Racist Comments Trigger International Condemnation'. *World Socialist Web Site (WSWS)*, January 13. www.wsws.org/en/articles/2018/01/13/inte-j13.html

Cohen, Claire. 2017. 'Donald Trump Sexism Tracker: Every Offensive Comment in One Place'. *The Telegraph*, July 14. www.telegraph.co.uk/women/politics/donald-trump-sexism-tracker-every-offensive-comment-in-one-place/amp/

Cole, Mike (ed). 1989. *Education for Equality: Some Guidelines for Good Practice*, London and New York, NY: Routledge.

Cole, Mike. 2008. *Marxism and Educational Theory: Origins and Issues*, London: Routledge.

Cole, Mike (ed). 2009. *Equality in the Secondary School: Promoting Good Practice Across the Curriculum*, London and New York, NY: Continuum.

Cole, Mike (ed). 2011a. *Equality in the Secondary School: Promoting Good Practice Acros308s the Curriculum*, London and New York, NY: Continuum.

Cole, Mike. 2011b. *Racism and Education in the U.K. and the U.S.: Towards a Socialist Alternative*, New York, NY and London: Palgrave Macmillan.

Cole, Mike. 2012. 'Capitalist Crisis and Fascism. Issues for Educational Practice'. In D. R. Cole (ed) *Surviving Economic Crisis Through Education*, New York, NY: Peter Lang.

Cole, Mike. 2016. *Racism: A Critical Analysis*, London: Pluto Press.

Cole, Mike. 2017a. *New Developments in Critical Race Theory and Education: Revisiting Racialized Capitalism and Socialism in Austerity*, New York, NY and London: Palgrave Macmillan.

Cole, Mike. 2017b. 'Critical Race Theory: A Marxist Critique'. In Michael Peters (ed) *Encyclopedia of Educational Philosophy and Theory, Volume 1*, Singapore: Springer, 301–308.

Cole, Mike (ed). 2018. *Education, Equality and Human Rights: Issues of Gender, 'Race', Sexuality, Disability and Social Class*, 4th Edition, London and New York, NY: Routledge.

Columbia University. 2018. 'America's Child Poverty Rate Remains Stubbornly High Despite Important Progress'. February 5. www.mailman.columbia.edu/public-health-now/news/america%E2%80%99s-child-poverty-rate-remains-stubbornly-high-despite-important-progress

Craemer, Thomas. 2015. 'Estimating Slavery Reparations: Present Value Comparisons of Historical Multigenerational Reparations Policies'. *Social Science Quarterly*, April 21. https://onlinelibrary.wiley.com/doi/full/10.1111/ssqu.12151

Dearden, Lizzie. 2017. 'Donald Trump Retweets Britain First Deputy Leader's Islamophobic Posts'. *Independent*, November 29. www.independent.co.uk/news/world/americas/us-politics/donald-trump-britain-first-retweet-muslim-migrants-jayda-fransen-deputy-leader-a8082001.html

Deaton, Angus. 2018. 'The U.S. Can No Longer Hide From Its Deep Poverty Problem'. *The New York Times*, January 24. www.nytimes.com/2018/01/24/opinion/poverty-united-states.html

de Menezes, Jack. 2017. 'Donald Trump "So Proud" of Nascar Plan to Sack Anyone that Protests Against National Anthem'. *The Independent*, September 25. www.independent.co.uk/sport/us-sport/donald-trump-president-protest-nascar-sack-drivers-twitter-nfl-take-a-knee-a7965846.html

Democratic Socialists of America. 2018. www.dsausa.org/

Dimaggio, Anthony. 2018. 'The Limits of #MeToo: Sectionalism, Economism, and "Identity Politics" on the Left'. *Counterpunch*, February 5. www.counterpunch.org/2018/02/05/the-limits-of-metoo-sectionalism-economism-and-identity-politics-on-the-left/

Elliott. 2018. www.cheatsheet.com/culture/cities-with-the-most-homeless-people.html/?a=viewall

Engels, Friedrich. 1955. *Anti-Dühring*, Chadwell Heath: Lawrence and Wishart.

Essif, Amien. 2018. 'Under Donald Trump, Socialism Seeps Into US Mainstream'. *DW*. www.dw.com/en/under-donald-trump-socialism-seeps-into-us-mainstream/a-42297787

Evans, Gavin. 2018. 'The Unwelcome Revival of "Race Science"'. *The Guardian*, March 2. www.theguardian.com/news/2018/mar/02/the-unwelcome-revival-of-race-science

Finley, Taryn. 2018. 'Trump Ignores Journalist's "Are You a Racist?" Question After Honoring Martin Luther King Jr'. *Huffpost*, January 13. www.huffingtonpost.co.uk/entry/trump-racist-question_us_5a58e3d7e4b02cebbfdb576f

Franklin, Jonathan. 2001. 'Chilean Army Admits 120 Thrown Into Sea'. *The Guardian*, January 9. www.theguardian.com/world/2001/jan/09/chile.pinochet

Fraser, Nancy. 2017. 'From Progressive Neoliberalism to Trump – and Beyond'. *American Affairs*, 1(4). https://americanaffairsjournal.org/2017/11/progressive-neoliberalism-trump-beyond/

Friedman, George. 2017. 'Presidential Constraints'. *Geopolitical Futures*, April 21. https://geopoliticalfutures.com/presidential-constraints/

Friends of the Earth. 2017. 'What Are Donald Trump's Policies on Climate Change and Other Environmental Issues?', September 5. https://friendsoftheearth.uk/climate-change/what-are-donald-trumps-policies-climate-change-and-other-environmental-issues?amp

Frostenson, Sarah. 2017. 'The Women's Marches May Have Been the Largest Demonstration in US History'. *Vox*, January 22. www.vox.com/2017/1/22/14350808/womens-marches-largest-demonstration-us-history-map

Fuchs, Christian. 2017. 'Donald Trump: A Critical Theory-Perspective on Authoritarian Capitalism'. *Communism, Capitalism and Critique*, 15(1). www.triple-c.at/index.php/tripleC/article/view/835/922

Gambino, Lauren and Laughland, Oliver. 2018. 'Donald Trump Signs Executive Order to End Family Separations'. *The Guardian*, June 20. https://theguardian.com/us-news/2018/jun/20/donald-trump-pledges-to-end-family-separations-by-executive-order

Garcia, Feliks. 2016. 'Ku Klux Klan Announces Donald Trump Victory Parade as White Supremacists Celebrate Nationwide'. *The Independent*, November 10. http://independent.co.uk/news/world/americas/ku-klux-klan-parade-north-carolina-donald-trump-celebration-president-elect-white-supremacists-alt-a7410671.html

Garner, Andra J., Mann, Michael E., Emanuel, Kerry A., Kopp, Robert E., Lin, Ning, Alley, Richard B., Horton, Benjamin P., DeConto, Robert M., Donnelly, Jeffery P. and Garner, David Pollard, edited by Chris Garrett. 2017. 'Impact of Climate Change on New York City's Coastal Flood Hazard: Increasing Flood Heights From the Preindustrial to 2300 CE'. *Proceedings of the National Academy of Sciences of the United States of America (PINAS) PNAS*, November, 114(45), 11861–11866. www.pnas.org/content/114/45/11861.full

Gasper, Phil. 2009. 'Reviving Socialism From Below'. *International Socialist Review*, 65, May. https://isreview.org/issue/65/reviving-socialism-below

Giroux, Henry A. 1998. 'Public Pedagogy and Rodent Politics: Cultural Studies and the Challenge of Disney'. *Arizona Journal of Hispanic Cultural Studies*, 2.

Giroux, Henry A. 1999. *The Mouse That Roared: Disney and the End of Innocence*, Lanham, MD: Rowman & Littlefield.

Giroux, Henry A. 2000. 'Public Pedagogy as Cultural Politics: Stuart Hall and the "Crisis" of Culture'. *Cultural Studies*, 14.

Giroux, Henry A. 2004. 'Cultural Studies, Public Pedagogy, and the Responsibility of Intellectuals'. *Communication and Critical/Cultural Studies*, 1(1).

Giroux, Henry A. 2010. *Hearts of Darkness: Torturing Children in the War on Terror*, London: Paradigm Publishers.

Giroux, Henry A. 2017. 'Fascism's Return and Trump's War on Youth'. *The Conversation*, December 14. https://theconversation.com/fascisms-return-and-trumps-war-on-youth-88867

Giroux, Henry A. 2018. '"Shithole Countries": Trump Uses the Rhetoric of Dictators'. *The Conversation*, January 12. https://theconversation.com/shithole-countries-trump-uses-the-rhetoric-of-dictators-89850

Glass, Andrew. 2008. 'Reagan Fires 11,000 Striking Air Traffic Controllers Aug. 5, 1981'. *Politico*, August 5. www.politico.com/story/2008/08/reagan-fires-11-000-striking-air-traffic-controllers-aug-5-1981-012292

Gold, Tanya. 2017. 'People Who Accuse Others of "Virtue Signalling" Are Trying to Stigmatise Empathy'. *New Statesman*, February 15. www.newstatesman.com/politics/uk/2017/02/people-who-accuse-others-virtue-signalling-are-trying-stigmatise-empathy

Goodman, H. A. 2017. '70 Percent of NFL Players Are Black Men. Colin Kaepernick Should Be Praised, Not Condemned'. *Huffington Post*, October 23. www. huffingtonpost.com/entry/70-of-nfl-players-are-black-men-colin-kaepernick_ us_57c7b12be4b07addc4114047

Graham, Bryan Armen. 2017. 'Donald Trump Blasts NFL Anthem Protesters: "Get that Son of a Bitch Off the Field"'. *The Guardian*, September 23. www.theguardian. com/sport/2017/sep/22/donald-trump-nfl-national-anthem-protests

Gramsci, Antonio. 1971. Selections From Prison Notebooks, London: Lawrence and Wishart

Gregory, Sean. 2016. 'Donald Trump Dismisses His "Locker-Room Talk" as Normal: Athletes Say It's Not'. *Time*, October 10. http://time.com/4526039/donald-trump-locker-room-athletes/

Griffiths, James and Smith-Spark, Laura. 2018. '"Shame on Trump!" World reacts to Trump's "shithole countries" remarks' CNN Politics January 12. https://edition. cnn.com/2018/01/12/politics/trump-shithole-countries-reaction-intl/index.html

Guardian Sport. 2017. 'Donald Trump Accuses NFL Players of "Total Disrespect" as Protests Continue'. *The Guardian*, October 23. www.theguardian.com/ sport/2017/oct/23/donald-trump-nfl-protests

Guardian Staff. 2017. 'Jeff Sessions Issues Directive Undercutting LGBT Protections'. *The Guardian*, October 6. www.theguardian.com/us-news/2017/oct/06/ jeff-sessions-issues-directive-undercutting-lgbtq-protections

Guardian Staff. 2018. 'How Trump's Budget Would Cut the Safety Net for the Poorest American'. *The Guardian*, February 13. www.theguardian.com/us-news/2018/ feb/13/trump-budget-cuts-safety-net-for-poorest-americans

Guest Writer (GW). 2017. 'Trump Will Be the Last Civic Nationalist'. *Altright.com*, October 26. https://altright.com/2017/10/26/trump-will-be-the-last-civic-nationalist/

Haberman, Maggie. 2016. 'Donald Trump Retweets Post With Quote From Mussolini'. *New York Times*, February 28. www.nytimes.com/politics/first-draft/2016/02/28/ donald-trump-retweets-post-likening-him-to-mussolini/

Haberman, Maggie and Oppel, Jr. Richard A. 2016. 'Donald Trump Criticizes Muslim Family of Slain U.S. Soldier, Drawing Ire'. *The New York Times*, July 30. www.nytimes.com/2016/07/31/us/politics/donald-trump-khizr-khan-wife-ghazala.html

Hamilton, Andrew. 2011. 'Herder's Theory of the Volksgeist'. Counter-Currents Publishing. www.counter-currents.com/2011/05/herders-theory-of-the-volksgeist/

Hamilton, D. 1999. 'The Pedagogic Paradox (or Why No Didactics in England?)'. *Pedagogy, Culture & Society*, 7(1), 135–152. www.tandfonline.com/doi/pdf/10. 1080/14681369900200048

Hansen, J., Johnson, D., Lacis, A., Lebedeff, S., Lee, P., Rind, D. and Russell, G. 198 1. 'Climate Impact of Increasing Atmospheric Carbon Dioxide'. *Science*, 213, 957–966.

Hardisty, Jean V. 1999. *Mobilizing Resentment: Conservative Resurgence From the John Birch Society to the Promise Keepers*, Boston, MA: Beacon Press. http:// jeanhardisty.com/writing/books/

Harriot, Michael. 2018. 'The Top 10 Racist Dog Whistles Hidden in Trump's State of the Union Address'. *The Root*, January 31. www.theroot.com/the-top-10-racist-dog-whistles-hidden-in-trumps-state-o-1822600239

Hartley-Parkinson, Richard. 2017. 'Britain First Holds "Security Training Day" to Teach How to Fight With Knives'. *Metro News*, July 11. http://metro.co.uk/2017/07/11/britain-first-holds-security-training-day-to-teach-how-to-fight-with-knives-6770167/amp/

Harvey, David. 2018. *Universal Alienation and the Real Subsumption of Daily Life Under Capital: A Response to Hardt and Negri*, New York, NY: City University of New York. www.triple-c.at/index.php/tripleC/article/view/1027/1197

Hayden, Michael Edison. 2018. 'Alt-Right Is Fractured, Violent Headed Into Trump's Second Year'. *Newsweek*, January 21. www.newsweek.com/alt-right-fractured-violent-headed-trump-second-year-785552?amp=1

Hayek, Frederick. 1960. *The Constitution of Liberty*, Chicago, IL: University of Chicago Press.

Helmore, Edward and Jacobs, Ben. 2015. 'Donald Trump's "Sexist" Attack on TV Debate Presenter Sparks Outrage'. *The Guardian*, August 9. www.theguardian.com/us-news/2015/aug/09/megyn-kelly-donald-trump-winner-republican-debate

Helsel, Phil and Smith, Saphora. 2018. 'President Trump Cancels London Trip, Blames Obama for Embassy Deal'. *NBC News*, January 12. www.nbcnews.com/politics/politics-news/president-trump-says-he-s-canceled-trip-london-n837036

Henderson, Barney. 2017. 'Donald Trump Says Both Sides to Blame for Charlottesville Violence and the "Alt-left" Bears Some Responsibility'. *The Telegraph*, August 16. http://telegraph.co.uk/news/2017/08/15/donald-trump-says-sides-charlottesville-violent/

Heyward, Anna. 2017. 'Since Trump's Victory, Democratic Socialists of America Has Become a Budding Political Force'. *The Nation*, December 21. www.thenation.com/article/in-the-year-since-trumps-victory-democratic-socialists-of-america-has-become-a-budding-political-force/

Hill, Libby. 2017. 'Trump's Inauguration Plans Too "Traditionally American" to Include Kanye West'. *Los Angeles Times*, January 19. www.latimes.com/entertainment/gossip/la-et-mg-kanye-west-donald-trump-inauguration-20170119-story.html

Hinks, Samir Karnik. 2012. 'What Is the Tendency of the Rate of Profit to Fall?'. *Socialist Review*, 371(July/August). http://socialistreview.org.uk/371/what-tendency-rate-profit-fall

Hirschfeld Davis, Julie. 2017. 'Trump Mocks Warren as "Pocahontas" at Navajo Veterans' Event'. *New York Times*, November 27. www.nytimes.com/2017/11/27/us/politics/trump-elizabeth-warren-pocahontas-navajo.html

Hitler, Adolph. 1925–1926. *Mein Kampf*, translated into English by James Murphy, A Project Gutenberg of Australia eBook, first posted September 2002. http://gutenberg.net.au/ebooks02/0200601.txt

Hjelmgaard, Kim. 2018. 'Vast Majority of New Wealth Last Year Went to Top 1%'. *USA Today*, January 22. www.usatoday.com/story/money/2018/01/22/vast-majority-new-wealth-last-year-went-top-1/1051947001/

Holloway, John. 1994. 'The Relevance of Marxism Today', *Common Sense: Journal of Edinburgh Conference of Socialist Economists*, No. 15 (April)

Holt, Jared. 2018. 'Richard Spencer: U.S. Military Should Have Enslaved Haitians After Hurricane Instead of Providing Relief'. *Right Wing Watch*, May 14. www.rightwingwatch.org/post/richard-spencer-u-s-military-should-have-enslaved-haitians-after-hurricane-instead-of-providing-relief/?utm_medium=email&utm_source=rww&utm_campaign=bestof

HOPENotHate. 2017. 'PatrikHermansson, MyYearInside theInternationalAlt-Right'. https://alternativeright.hopenothate.com/my-year-inside-the-international-alt-right

Hughes,Trevor.2018. '"AltRight"LeaderRichardSpencerSaysHisRalliesAren't"Fun" Anymore'. *USA Today*, March 12. www.usatoday.com/story/news/2018/03/12/alt-right-leader-richard-spencer-says-his-rallies-arent-fun-anymore/416579002/

Hunter, Paul. 2017. 'Trump the "First Step" Toward Identity Politics: Richard Spencer'. *CBC News*, January 18. http://cbc.ca/news/world/richard-spencer-trump-identity-politics-1.3940205

The Independent. 2008. 'The Full Text of Barack Obama's Victory Speech'. *The Independent*, November 5. www.independent.co.uk/news/world/americas/the-full-text-of-barack-obamas-victory-speech-993008.html

Inequality.org. 2018. 'Global Inequality'. https://inequality.org/facts/global-inequality/

International Centre for Public Pedagogy (ICPUP). 2018. London: University of East London. www.uel.ac.uk/schools/cass/research/the-international-centre-for-public-pedagogy

International Socialist Organisation. 2018. 'About Us'. www.internationalsocialist.org/about-us/

International Youth and Students for Social Equality. 2018. 'A Socialist Strategy Is Needed to Defend Immigrants!'. *World Socialist Web Site (WSWS)*, January 27. www.wsws.org/en/articles/2018/01/27/immi-j27.html

Jenkins, Nash. 2018. 'Counter-Protesters Dwarfed a White Nationalist Rally in Washington'. *Time*, August 13. http://time.com/longform/charlottesville-unite-right-washington-protest/

Johnson, Kevin. 2018. 'Trump's Path to Citizenship for 1.8 Million Will Leave Out Nearly HalfofAllDreamers'. *The Conversation*, January 30. http://theconversation.com/trumps-path-to-citizenship-for-1-8-million-will-leave-out-nearly-half-of-all-dreamers-90899

Kapko, Matt. 2016, November 3. 'Twitter's Impact on 2016 Presidential Election Is Unmistakable'. *CIO*. http://cio.com/article/3137513/social-networking/twitters-impacton-2016-presidential-election-is-unmistakable.html

Kentish, Benjamin. 2017a. 'Donald Trump Is a Psychopath, Suffers Psychosis and Is an "Enormous Present Danger", Says Psychiatrist'. *Independent*, November 30. www.independent.co.uk/news/world/americas/us-politics/donald-trump-psychopath-psychosis-mental-health-danger-us-president-goldwater-rule-psychiatrist-a8084726.html

Kentish, Benjamin. 2017b. 'Donald Trump "Kept Book of Adolf Hitler's Speeches in His Bedside Cabinet"'. *Independent*, March 20. www.independent.co.uk/news/world/americas/us-politics/donald-trump-adolf-hitler-books-bedside-cabinet-ex-wife-ivana-trump-vanity-fair-1990-a7639041.html

Kerr, Donna H. 1999. 'Voicing Democracy in an Imperfect World: Towards a Public Pedagogy of Nurture'. In F. Smith and G. D. Fenstermacher (eds) *Leadership for Educational Renewal: Developing a Cadre of Leaders. Agenda for Education in Democracy*, Vol. 1. San Francisco, CA: Jossey-Bass.

Klein, Betsy and Schleifer, Theodore. 2015. 'What's in a Retweet? Donald Trump Explains'. *CNN Politics*, August 26. http://edition.cnn.com/2015/08/25/politics/donald-trump-retweets-iowa/

Know Your Meme. 2018. http://knowyourmeme.com/memes/tendies-stories

Krieg, Gregory. 2017. 'The 14 Most Shocking Comments From Trump's Charlottesville News Conference'. *CNN Politics*, August 16. http://edition.cnn.com/2017/08/15/politics/donald-trump-charlottesville-lines/index.html

Lartey, Jamiles. 2017. 'Is Meals on Wheels About to Become a Fatality of Trump's Budget?'. *The Guardian*, March 17. https://theguardian.com/commentisfree/2017/mar/17/meals-on-wheels-fatality-trumps-budget

Laughland, Oliver. 2017. 'Inspired By Matin Luther King Jr, a New Civil Rights Leader Takes Center Stage'. *The Guardian*, October 25. www.theguardian.com/us-news/2017/oct/25/william-barber-martin-luther-king-jr-civil-rights-leader

Lawson, Max. 2016. 'It's Time to Demolish the Myth of Trickle-down Economics'. Geneva: World Economic Forum, July 19. www.weforum.org/agenda/2016/07/it-s-time-to-demolish-the-myth-of-trickle-down-economics/

Lennard, Natasha. 2018. 'Is Antifa Counterproductive? White Nationalist Richard Spencer Would Beg to Differ'. *The Intercept*, March 17. https://theintercept.com/2018/03/17/richard-spencer-college-tour-antifa-alt-right/

Leonhardt, David and Philbrickjan, Ian Prasad. 2018. 'Donald Trump's Racism: The Definitive List'. *New York Times*, January 15. www.nytimes.com/interactive/2018/01/15/opinion/leonhardt-trump-racist.html?smid=tw-share&mtrref=t.co&assetType=opinion

Liberation. undated. 'About the PSL'. www.liberationnews.org/home-page/about/

Lind, Dara. 2015. 'Donald Trump Proposes "Total and Complete Shutdown of Muslims Entering the United States"'. *Vox*, December 7. www.vox.com/2015/12/7/9867900/donald-trump-muslims

Lion, Patrick and Mortimer, Caroline. 2017. 'Teen Racially Abused on Train Thanks Men Who Were Stabbed to Death "Saving Her Life"'. *The Mirror*, May 30. www.mirror.co.uk/news/world-news/teen-racially-abused-train-thanks-10526561

Liptak, Kevin and Jones, Athena. 2017. 'With Latest Jabs, Trump-Obama Relationship Reaches Historic Nastiness'. *CNN Politics*, September 3. http://edition.cnn.com/2017/06/28/politics/trump-obama-relationship/index.html

Lockhart, P. R. 2018. 'Trump Says He Deserves Credit for the Lowest Black Unemployment Rate in Decades. He doesn't'. *Vox*, January 18. www.vox.com/platform/amp/policy-and-politics/2018/1/18/16902390/trump-black-unemployment-rate-record-decline

London, Eric. 2018a. 'Trump Unveils Sweeping Attack on Immigrants in Reform Proposal'. *World Socialist Web Site (WSWS)*, January 30. www.wsws.org/en/articles/2018/01/30/immi-j30.html

London, Eric. 2018b. 'Trump's Reign of Terror on California Immigrants'. *World Socialist Web Site (WSWS)*, February 27. www.wsws.org/en/articles/2018/02/27/pers-f27.html

London, Eric. 2018c. 'US Denies Right to Asylum'. *World Socialist Web Site (WSWS)*, May 3. www.wsws.org/en/articles/2018/05/03/pers-m03.html

London, Eric. 2018d. 'The International Significance of the March for Our Lives Demonstrations'. *World Socialist Web Site (WSWS)*, March 26. www.wsws.org/en/articles/2018/03/26/pers-m26.html

Lorius Claude et al. 1985. 'A 150,000-Year Climatic Record From Antarctic Ice'. *Nature*, 316, 591–596.

Los Angeles Times. ongoing. 'Everything President Trump Has Tweeted (and What It Was About)'. www.latimes.com/politics/la-pol-updates-everything-president-trump-has-tweeted-and-what-it-was-about-2017-htmlstory.html

Lusher, Adam. 2018. 'Neo-Nazis Say Donald Trump's "Sh**hole Countries" Comments Show How He Thinks Like Them'. *The Independent*, January 13. www.independent.co.uk/news/world/americas/us-politics/donald-trump-shithole-countries-neo-nazis-white-supremacists-celebrate-more-or-less-same-page-racist-a8157796.html

Mahdawi, Arwa. 2018. 'Socialism Is No Longer a Dirty Word in the US and That's Scary for Some'. *The Guardian*, July 29. https://theguardian.com/commentisfree/2018/jul/29/socialism-no-longer-dirty-word-us-scary-for-some

Main, Douglas. 2015. 'Slavery Reparations Could Cost Up to $14 Trillion, According to New Calculation'. *Newsweek*, August 19. www.newsweek.com/slavery-reparations-could-cost-14-trillion-according-new-calculation-364141

Maisuria, Alpesh. 2016. 'Class Struggle in Cultural Formation in Contemporary Times: A Focus on the Theoretical Importance of Antonio Gramsci and the Organic Intellectualism of Russell Brand'. *Knowledge Cultures*, 6.

Maisuria, Alpesh. 2018. *Class Consciousness and Education in Sweden: A Marxist Analysis for Revolutionary Strategy in a Social Democracy*, New York, NY and London: Routledge.

Maisuria, Alpesh and Cole, Mike. 2017. 'The Neoliberalization of Higher Education in England: An Alternative Is Possible'. *Policy Futures in Education*, 15(5).

Mann, Michael 1997. 'The Contradictions of Continuous Revolution'. In I. Kershaw and M. Lewin (eds) *Stalinism and Nazism: Dictatorship in Comparison*, Cambridge: Cambridge University Press.

Mann, Michael. 2004. *Fascists*, Cambridge: Cambridge University Press.

Mann, Michael E. 2018. 'When It Comes to Climate Change, Donald Trump Has Nothing to Fear But Trump Himself'. *The Ecologist*, January 30. https://theecologist.org/2018/jan/30/when-it-comes-climate-change-donald-trump-has-nothing-fear-trump-himself

Mark, Michelle. 2017a. 'Trump Reportedly Said Haitians "All Have AIDS" and Nigerians Live in "Huts" During Outburst on Immigration'. *Business Insider*, *UK*, December 23. http://uk.businessinsider.com/trump-reportedly-said-haitians-have-aids-nigerians-live-in-huts-in-immigration-outburst-2017-12

Mark, Michelle. 2017b. 'The Chilling Worldview of a White Supremacist Who Helped Lead the Charlottesville Rally Shows Why So Many People Are Furious With Trump'. *Business Insider*, August 16. http://uk.businessinsider.com/why-people-are-furious-with-trump-charlottesville-white-supremacist-vice-video-2017-8?r=US&IR=T

Martin, Patrick. 2017. 'Behind Trump's Attack on the NFL Football Players'. *World Socialist Web Site (WSWS)*, September 26. www.wsws.org/en/articles/2017/09/26/pers-s26.html

Martin, Patrick. 2018a. 'US to Deport 262,000 Salvadoran Immigrants'. *World Socialist Web Site (WSWS)*, January 9. www.wsws.org/en/articles/2018/01/09/pers-j09.html

Martin, Patrick. 2018b. 'Bannon Attack on Trump White House Fuels Washington Political Warfare'. *World Socialist Web Site (WSWS)*, January 5. www.wsws.org/en/articles/2018/01/05/bann-j05.html

Marx, Karl. 1894 [1966] *Capital Volume 3*, Moscow: Progress Publishers

Maza, Cristina. 2017. 'Moments White Supremacists, Neo-Nazis and the Alt-right Marched on America in 2017, in Images'. *Newsweek*, December 27. www.newsweek.com/white-supremacists-neo-nazis-alt-right-march-america-2017-760514?amp=1

Mazelis, Fred. 2017. 'Trump Retweets Fascist Anti-Muslim Videos From Britain'. *World Socialist Web Site (WSWS)*, November 30. www.wsws.org/en/articles/2017/11/30/trum-n30.html

McLaren, Peter. 2013. 'Seeds of Resistance: Towards a Revolutionary Critical Ecopedagogy'. *Socialist Studies/Études socialistes*, 9(1), Spring.

McLaren, Peter. 2018. 'Foreword: The Wretched State'. In Mike Cole (ed) *Education, Equality and Human Rights: Issues of Gender, 'Race', Sexuality, Disability and Social Class*, 4th Edition, London and New York, NY: Routledge.

McVeigh, Rory. 1999. 'Structural Incentives for Conservative Mobilization: Power Devaluation and the Rise of the Ku Klux Klan, 1915–1925'. *Social Forces*, 77(4), June.

McVeigh, Rory. 2009. *The Rise of the Ku Klux Klan: Right-Wing Movements and National Politics*, Minneapolis, MN: University of Minnesota Press.

Meenakshi, Jagadeesan. 2018a. 'Trump Administration to Add Citizenship Question to US Census'. *World Socialist Web Site (WSWS)*, March 29. www.wsws.org/en/articles/2018/03/29/cens-m29.html

Meenakshi, Jagadeesan. 2018b. 'US Immigration Service Quietly Removes "Nation of Immigrants" From Its Mission Statement'. *World Socialist Web Site (WSWS)*, February 26. www.wsws.org/en/articles/2018/02/26/ucis-f26.html

MeToo. undated. https://metoomvmt.org

Michel, Lincoln. 2018. 'Netflix's *Trump: An American Dream* Shows the President Has Always Been Like This', April 7. www.gq.com/story/netflix-trump-an-american-dream

Milam, Greg. 2017. 'Donald Trump Tests Eight 30ft High Walls for Border With Mexico'. *Sky News*, December 27. http://news.sky.com/story/donald-trump-tests-eight-30ft-high-walls-for-border-with-mexico-11186092

Miller, Zeke and Colvin, Jill. 2018. 'Trump Stands by "Culture" Criticism of European Immigration'. *Associated Press*, July 13. https://apnews.com/ddeba6e1c7294aef8cf49ae9494c42dd

Mindock, Clark. 2017. 'Billy Bush Says Trump's Notorious "Grabbing" Commen "Wasn'tLockerRoomTalk"'. *The Independent*, May 22. www.independent.co.uk/news/world/americas/us-politics/trump-grabbing-access-hollwood-tapes-billy-bush-not-locker-room-talk-a7750376.html

Moisio, Olli-Pekka and Suoranta, Juha. 2006. *Education and the Spirit of Time*. Rotterdam, Netherlands: Sense.

Monbiot, George. 2016. 'Neoliberalism: The Deep Story That Lies Beneath Donald Trump's Triumph'. *The Guardian*, November 14. www.theguardian.com/commentisfree/2016/nov/14/neoliberalsim-donald-trump-george-monbiot

Morris, Chris. 2018. 'Here's How Many People Participated in Women's Marches This Year'. *Fortune*, January 22. http://fortune.com/2018/01/22/womens-march-2018-numbers/

Mostrom, Anthony. 2017. 'The Fascist and the Preacher: Gerald L. K. Smith and Francis Parker Yockey in Cold War – Era Los Angeles'. *Los Angeles Review of Books*, May 13. https://lareviewofbooks.org/article/the-fascist-and-the-preacher-gerald-l-k-smith-and-francis-parker-yockey-in-cold-war-era-los-angeles/#

Nahdee, Ali. 2017. 'Disney Exec: "She Has to Be Sexy" Historical Inaccuracies and Harms of Disney's Pocahontas'. *Indian Country Today*, August 12. https://indiancountrymedianetwork.com/culture/arts-entertainment/disney-exec-sexy-historical-inaccuracies-harms-disneys-pocahontas/

National Policy Institute a Call for Papers By Evan McLaren. 2017. 'Putting the Policy in the National Policy Institute'. https://nationalpolicy.institute/2017/12/16/a-call-for-papers/

Neiwert, David. 2017. 'Birth of the Alt Right'. *Political Research Associates*, March 22. www.politicalresearch.org/2017/03/22/birth-of-the-alt-right/#sthash.kwYdxgdL.dpbs

Nelson, Libby and Swanson, Kelly. 2017. 'Full Transcript: Donald Trump's Press Conference Defending the Charlottesville Rally'. *Vox*, August 15. www.vox.com/2017/8/15/16154028/trump-press-conference-transcript-charlottesville

Newport, Frank. 2018. 'Democrats More Positive About Socialism Than Capitalism'. Washington, DC: Gallup, August 13. https://news.gallup.com/poll/240725/democrats-positive-socialism-capitalism.aspx

O'Brien, Luke. 2017. 'The Making of an American Nazi'. *The Atlantic*, December. www.theatlantic.com/magazine/archive/2017/12/the-making-of-an-american-nazi/544119/

O'Connor, Maureen. 2017. 'The Philosophical Fascists of the Gay Alt-Right'. *The Cut*, April 30. www.thecut.com/2017/04/jack-donovan-philosophical-fascists-of-the-gay-alt-right.html

Oliver, Scott. 2017. 'Unwrapping the Conspiracy Theory at the Heart of the Alt-Right'. *Vice*, February 23. www.vice.com/en_uk/article/78mnny/unwrapping-the-conspiracy-theory-that-drives-the-alt-right

One Billion Rising. 2018. www.onebillionrising.org/about/campaign/

O'Toole, Fintan. 2018. 'Trial Runs for Fascism Are in Full Flow'. *The Irish Times*, June 26. https://irishtimes.com/opinion/fintan-o-toole-trial-runs-for-fascism-are-in-full-flow-1.3543375

Ott, Brian L. 2017. 'The Age of Twitter: Donald J. Trump and the Politics of Debasement'. *Critical Studies in Media Communication*, 34(1), 59–68.

Our Revolution. undated. 'Our Mission'. https://ourrevolution.com/about/

Oxfam. 2018. 'Reward Work, Not Wealth: To End the Inequality Crisis, We Must Build an Economy for Ordinary Working People, Not the Rich and Powerful'. https://policy-practice.oxfam.org.uk/publications/reward-work-not-wealth-to-end-the-inequality-crisis-we-must-build-an-economy-fo-620396

Paxton, Robert O. 2004. *The Anatomy of Fascism*, New York, NY: Alred A. Knopf.

Paxton, Robert O. 2017. 'American Duce. Is Donald Trump a Fascist or a Plutocrat?'. *Harper's Magazine*, November 1. https://harpers.org/archive/2017/05/american-duce/

People's Congress of Resistance. 2017. 'Inaugural People's Congress of Resistance Draws Together Grassroots Leaders Unified By a Revolutionary Vision'. www.congressofresistance.org/inaugural_people_s_congress_of_resistance_draws_together_grassroots_leaders_unified_by_a_revolutionary_vision

People's Congress of Resistance. undated a. *Society for the Many: A Vision for Revolution [Manifesto]Manifesto of the People's Congress of Resistance*. www.congressofresistance.org/society_for_the_many_a_vision_for_revolution

People's Congress of Resistance. undated b. *Call to Action*. www.congressofresistance.org/call_to_action

Phillips, Amber. 2017. '"They're Rapists", President Trump's Campaign Launch Speech Two Years Later Annotated'. *The Washington Post*, June 16. www.washingtonpost.com/news/the-fix/wp/2017/06/16/theyre-rapists-presidents-trump-campaign-launch-speech-two-years-later-annotated/?utm_term=.ae928cae82eb

Phillips, Whitney. 2016. *This Is Why We Can't Have Nice Things: Mapping the Relationship Between Online Trolling and Mainstream Culture*, Cambridge, MA: The MIT Press.

Politico Staff. 2017. 'Full Text: Trump's 2017 U.N. Speech Transcript'. *Politico*, September 19. http://politico.com/story/2017/09/19/trump-un-speech-2017-full-text-transcript-242879

Polyani, Karl. 1944. *The Great Transformation*, New York, NY: Farrar and Rinehart.

Poor People's Campaign. undated. https://poorpeoplescampaign.org/index.php/fundamental-principles/

Rachmen, Gideon. 2017. 'Donald Trump Is More Than a Blip in History'. *Financial Times*, October 9.

Raghian, Ardalan. 2018. 'Newly Released Documents Show Dakota Access Pipeline Is Discriminatory Against Indigenous People'. *Truthout*, January 22. www.truth-out.org/news/item/43294-newly-released-documents-show-dakota-access-pipeline-is-discriminatory-against-native-americans

Ransby, Barbara. 2015. 'The Class Politics of Black Lives Matter'. *Dissent*. www.dissentmagazine.org/article/class-politics-black-lives-matter

Redneck Revolt. undated(a). www.redneckrevolt.org/

Redneck Revolt. undated(b). *Organising Principles*. www.redneckrevolt.org/principles

Reese, Ashley. 2018. 'Donald Trump Wants Congressional Term Limits and to Be President Forever'. *The Slot*, May 11. https://theslot.jezebel.com/trump-wants-congressional-term-limits-and-to-be-preside-1825955371

Rehagen, Tony. 2017. 'Matthew Heimbach Has a Dream – A *Very* Different Dream'. *Indianapolis Monthly*, April. www.indianapolismonthly.com/features/white-space/.

Renton, Dave. 1999. *Fascism: Theory and Practice*, London: Pluto Press. www.e-reading.club/bookreader.php/135772/Fascism_-_theory_and_practice.pdf

Rikowski, Glenn. 2001. 'The Importance of Being a Radical Educator in Capitalism Today'. Paper presented at a Guest Lecture in Sociology of Education, The Gillian Rose Room, University of Warwick, Coventry, May 31.

Rikowski, Glenn. 2006. 'Education and the Politics of Human Resistance'. *Information for Social Change*, 23, Summer. www.academia.edu/5997035/Education_and_the_Politics_of_Human_Resistance

Rikowski, Glenn. 2018. 'Crisis and Education'. A presentation at the International Seminar for Public Pedagogies (ICPuP), University of East London, Stratford Campus, February 21.

Rikowski, Glenn. forthcoming, 2019. 'No Abstract Acts of Kindness: Communism as a Suppressed Form of Life in Contemporary Society'. A paper prepared for Sixteenth Historical Materialism London Conference.

Rikowski, Glenn and Ocampo Gonzalez, Aldo. 2018. 'Interview on Marxism, Critical Pedagogy and Inclusive Education: Discussions for a Revolutionary Discourse (Glenn Rikowski Interviewed by Aldo Ocampo Gonzalez), the Center for Latin American Studies on Inclusive Education (CELEI), March. https://www.celei.cl/wp-content/uploads/2018/03/Entrevista-sobre-Marximo-Pedagog%C3%ADDa-Cr%C3%ADtica-y-Educaci%C3%B3n-Inclusiva_Dr.-Glenn-Rikowski_UK.pdf

Rowell, Alex and Hanion, Seth. 2017. 'The Final Tax Bill Is a Bigger Win for Foreign Investors Than the Entire Working and Middle Class in Trump States'. Washington DC: Center for American Progress, December 19. www.americanprogress.org/issues/economy/news/2017/12/19/444363/final-tax-bill-bigger-win-foreign-investors-entire-working-middle-class-trump-states/

Ruptly. 2017. 'LIVE: Alt-right Figure Richard Spencer Holds Speech at University of Florida Among Protesters Streamed Live on Oct 19 2017'. www.youtube.com/watch?v=u2XvwcNSDmw

Rushe, Dominic. 2018. 'As State of the Union Nears, Is America Great Again for the Working Class?'. *The Guardian*, January 25. www.theguardian.com/us-news/2018/jan/25/trump-state-of-union-workers-rights-working-class-record

Sandlin, Jennifer A., O'Malley, Michael, P. and Burdick, Jake. 2011. 'Mapping the Complexity of Public Pedagogy Scholarship: 1894–2010'. *Review of Educational Research*, September, 338–375.

Sandlin, Jennifer A., Schultz, Brian D. and Burdick, Jake. 2010. *Handbook of Public Pedagogy*, New York, NY: Routledge.

Savage, Michael. 2018. 'Richest 1% on Target to Own Two-thirds of All Wealth By 2030'. *The Observer*, April 8.

Segal, Oren. 2016. 'Pepe the Frog: Yes, a Harmless Cartoon Can Become an Alt-right'. *The Guardian*, September 29. https://theguardian.com/commentisfree/2016/sep/29/pepe-the-frog-alt-right-mascot-racist-anti-semitic

Selfa, Lance. 2018a. 'The Phony "Populist" Delivers for the Rich'. *Socialist Worker*, January 4. https://socialistworker.org/2018/01/04/the-phony-populist-delivers-for-the-rich

Selfa, Lance. 2018b. *U.S Politics in an Age of Uncertainty*, Chicago, IL: Haymarket Books.

Seymour, Richard. 2016. 'Schadenfreude With Bite'. *London Review of Books*, 38(24), December 15, 11–14. www.lrb.co.uk/v38/n24/richard-seymour/schadenfreude-with-bite

Shabi, Rachel. 2017. 'Is This Really How Fascism Takes Hold in the US?'. *Aljazeera*, February 8. http://aljazeera.com/indepth/opinion/2017/02/fascism-takes-hold-170207142614174.html

Shaefer, H. Luke and Edin, Kathryn. 2018 'Welfare Reform and the Families It Left Behind'. *Pathways*, Winter.

Shapiro, Ben. 2016. 'Why Trump Fans Keep Using the Slur "Globalist"'. *The Daily Wire*, August 2. www.dailywire.com/news/8024/why-trump-fans-keep-using-slur-globalist-ben-shapiro#

Shearer, Elisa and Gottfried, Jeffrey. 2017. 'News Use Across Social Media Platforms 2017'. Washington, DC: Pew Center. www.journalism.org/2017/09/07/news-use-across-social-media-platforms-2017/

Shekhovtsov, Anton. 2017. 'The "Alt-right" Has Died in Charlottesville, as a Term'. *Anton Shekhovtsov's Blog*. August 13. http://anton-shekhovtsov.blogspot.co.uk/2017/08/the-alt-right-died-in-charlottesville.html

Shilton, Jordan. 2016. 'Bernie Sanders and the "Scandinavian Model"'. *World Socialist Web Site (WSWS)*, February 26. www.wsws.org/en/articles/2016/02/26/scan-f26.html

Shugerman, Emily. 2018. 'Warren Addresses Trump's "Pocahontas" Slur and Controversy Over Her Heritage in Surprise Speech to Native American Leaders'. *The Independent*, February 14. www.independent.co.uk/news/world/americas/us-politics/warren-trump-native-american-pocahontas-claims-cherokee-heritage-national-congress-of-american-a8211306.html

Simon, Mallory. 2018. 'Neo-Nazi Troll Storm Was Crude But Not a Threat, White Supremacist Argues'. *CNN*, January 16. https://edition.cnn.com/2018/01/16/us/andrew-anglin-gersh-lawsuit-filing/index.html

Simon, Roger. 1992. *Teaching Against the Grain: Texts for a Pedagogy of Possibility*, Westport, CT: Bergin and Garvey.

Simon, Roger. 1995. 'Broadening the Vision of University-Based Study of Education: The Contribution of Cultural Studies'. *The Review of Education/Pedagogy/Cultural Studies* 12(1).

Singal, Jesse. 2017 'Undercover With the Alt-Right'. *The New York Times*, September 19. www.nytimes.com/2017/09/19/opinion/alt-right-white-supremacy-undercover.html?mcubz=1

Sky News. 2018. 'Donald Trump Warns North Korean Leader Kim Jong Un: My Button Is Much Bigger Than Yours'. *Sky News*, January 3. https://news.sky.com/story/my-button-is-much-bigger-trump-threatens-north-korea-with-nuclear-war-11193800

Smith, David. 2018a. 'Trump Defends Top Official Accused of Domestic Abuse: 'He Did a Very Good Job'. *The Guardian*, February 8. www.theguardian.com/us-news/2018/feb/09/trump-defends-rob-porter-accused-of-domestic-abuse?CMP=Share_iOSApp_Other

Smith, David. 2018b. '50 Years After Martin Luther King's Death, a "New King" Fights for Justice'. *The Guardian*, April 3. www.theguardian.com/us-news/2018/apr/03/william-barber-martin-luther-king-mlk-50th-anniversary-new-king?CMP=Share_iOSApp_Other

Smith, Heather and Smith, Mark K. 2008 . *The Art of Helping Others: Being Around, Being There, Being Wise*, London: Jessica Kingsley Publishers.

Smith, Lydia. 2018. 'Neo-Nazi Behind Daily Stormer Website Andrew "Weev" Auernheimer "Is of Jewish Descent, His Mother Says"'. *The Independent*, January

4. www.independent.co.uk/news/world/americas/neo-nazi-daily-stormer-troll-jewish-descent-anti-semitic-andrew-auernheimer-weev-a8140946.html?amp

Smith, Mark K. 2012. 'What Is Pedagogy?'. *The Encyclopaedia of Informal Education*. http://infed.org/mobi/what-is-pedagogy/

Solon, Olivia. 2016. 'Facebook's Failure: Did Fake News and Polarized Politics Get Trump Elected?'. *The Guardian*, November 10. https://theguardian.com/technology/2016/nov/10/facebook-fake-news-election-conspiracy-theories?CMP = oth_b-aplnews_d-1

Southern Poverty Law Center (SPLC). 2012. 'Misogyny: The Sites'. *Montgomery, Al: SPLC*, March 1. www.splcenter.org/fighting-hate/intelligence-report/2012/misogyny-sites

Southern Poverty Law Center (SPLC). 2017. 'Christopher Cantwell'. *Montgomery. Al:SPLC.* www.splcenter.org/fighting-hate/extremist-files/individual/christopher-cantwell

Southern Poverty Law Center (SPLC). undated. 'Augustus Sol Invictus'. *Montgomery, Al: SPLC.* www.splcenter.org/fighting-hate/extremist-files/individual/augustus-sol-invictus

Sparks, Grace. 2018. 'Americans Are Split in Half on National Anthem Protests'. *CNN Politics*, June 5. https://cnn.com/2018/06/05/politics/anthem-protest-polling/index.html

Spencer, Richard. 2018. 'Video: "College Tour Course Correction"'. *Alt-Right.com*. https://altright.com/2018/03/11/college-tour-course-correction/

Spillar, Kathy. 'The 2018 Women's Marches By the Numbers'. *Ms Magazine*, March 13. http://msmagazine.com/blog/2018/03/13/2018-womens-marches-numbers/

Squirrell, Tim. 2017. 'Linguistic Data Analysis of 3 Billion Reddit Comments Shows the Alt-right Is Getting Stronger'. *Quartz*, August 18. https://qz.com/1056319/what-is-the-alt-right-a-linguistic-data-analysis-of-3-billion-reddit-comments-shows-a-disparate-group-that-is-quickly-uniting/

Stern, Ken. 2016. 'Exclusive: Stephen Bannon, Trump's New C.E.O., Hints at His Master Plan'. *Vanity Fair*, August 17. www.vanityfair.com/news/2016/08/breitbart-stephen-bannon-donald-trump-master-plan

Sunshine, Spencer. 2017. 'Three Pillars of the Alt Right: White Nationalism, Antisemitism, and Misogyny'. *Political Research Associates*, December 4. www.politicalresearch.org/2017/12/04/three-pillars-of-the-alt-right-white-nationalism-antisemitism-and-misogyny/#sthash.j17ilx5f.dpbs

Tait, Amelia. 2016. 'The Strange Case of Marina Joyce and Internet Hysteria'. *The Guardian*, August 4. https://theguardian.com/technology/2016/aug/04/marina-joyce-internethysteria-witch-hunts-cyberspace?CMP = oth_b-aplnews_d-1

Tastrom, Katie. 2018. 'Trump's New Medicaid Work Requirements Are a Disaster for Disabled People' (and everyone else). *Think*, January 12. www.nbcnews.com/think/opinion/trump-s-new-medicaid-work-requirements-are-disaster-disabled-people-ncna836991

Tax Policy Center. 2017a. 'Distributional Analysis of the Conference Agreement for the Tax Cuts and Jobs Act'. December 18. www.taxpolicycenter.org/publications/distributional-analysis-conference-agreement-tax-cuts-and-jobs-act

Tax Policy Center. 2017b. 'T17–0316 – Conference Agreement: The Tax Cuts and Jobs Act; Baseline: Current Law; Distribution of Federal Tax Change By Expanded Cash Income Percentile, 2027'. December 18. www.taxpolicycenter.org/model-estimates/conference-agreement-tax-cuts-and-jobs-act-dec-2017/t17-0316-conference-agreement

Thelwall, Mike, Buckley, Kevan, and Paltoglou, Georgios. 2011. 'Sentiment in Twitter Events'. *Journal of the American Society for Information Science and Technology*, 62(2), 406–418.

Thomas-Peter, Hannah. 2018a. 'Explosive Book Claims – And What They Mean for Donald Trump'. *Sky News*, January 4. http://news.sky.com/story/a-moment-of-peril-for-the-white-house-occupant-11194840

Thomas-Peter, Hannah. 2018b 'Fascist Fighters or Criminals? On the Streets With Portland's Antifa Group'. *Sky News*, January 22. https://news.sky.com/story/fascist-fighters-or-criminals-on-the-streets-with-portlands-antifa-group-11217880

Trend, David. 1992. *Cultural Pedagogy: Art/Education/Politics*, Westport, CT: Bergin and Garvey.

Trump Twitter Archive. ongoing. www.trumptwitterarchive.com/

United States Holocaust Memorial Museum. 2018a. 'The Murder of the Handicapped'. www.ushmm.org/outreach/en/article.php?ModuleId=10007683

United States Holocaust Memorial Museum. 2018b. 'Euthanasia Program'. www.ushmm.org/wlc/mobile/en/article.php?ModuleId=10005200

United States Holocaust Memorial Museum. 2018c. 'Prisoners of the Camps'. www.ushmm.org/outreach/en/article.php?ModuleId=10007754

Verginella, Marta. 2011. 'Antislavismo, razzismo di frontiera?'. Aut aut 349.

Vice News. 2017. 'Race and Terror – VICE News Tonight (HBO)', *New York: Vice News*. https://int.search.myway.com/search/video.jhtml?n=78489219&p2=%5EC P6%5Exdm259%5ETTAB02%5Egb&pg=video&pn=1&ptb=D63A1AF6-6331-4931-8AAC-94838A9B6676&qs=&searchfor=charlottesville+rally&si=37&ss=sub&st=tab&tpr=sbt&trs=wtt

Wagner, Meg. 2017. '"Blood and Soil": Protesters Chant Nazi Slogan in Charlottesville'. *CNN*, August 12. http://edition.cnn.com/2017/08/12/us/charlottesville-unite-the-right-rally/index.html

Walter, Karla and Rowell, Alex. 2018 'President Trump's Policies Are Hurting American Workers'. Washington, DC: Center for American Progress Action Fund, January 26. www.americanprogressaction.org/issues/economy/reports/2018/01/26/168366/president-trumps-policies-hurting-american-workers/

Walters, Joanna. 2017a. 'What Is Daca and Who Are the Dreamers?'. *The Guardian*, September 14. www.theguardian.com/us-news/2017/sep/04/donald-trump-what-is-daca-dreamers

Walters, Joanna. 2017b. 'Neo-Nazis, White Nationalists, and Internet Trolls: Who's Who in the Far Right'. *The Guardian*, August 17. www.theguardian.com/world/2017/aug/17/charlottesville-alt-right-neo-nazis-white-nationalists

Walters, Joanna. 2018. 'Trump University: Court Upholds $25m Settlement to Give Students' Money Back'. *The Guardian*, February 6. www.theguardian.com/us-news/2018/feb/06/trump-university-court-upholds-25m-settlement-to-give-students-money-back

Watt, Celia Saixue. 2017. 'Redneck Revolt: The Armed Leftwing Group that Wants to Stamp Out Fascism'. *The Guardian*, July 11. www.theguardian.com/us-news/2017/jul/11/redneck-revolt-guns-anti-racism-fascism-far-left

Weaver, Matthew, Booth, Robert and Jacobs, Ben with additional reporting by Jon Henley and Daniel Boffey. 2017. 'Theresa May Condemns Trump's Retweets of UK Far-right Leader's Anti-Muslim Videos'. *The Guardian*, November 29. www.theguardian.com/us-news/2017/nov/29/trump-account-retweets-anti-muslim-videos-of-british-far-right-leader?CMP=Share_iOSApp_Other

Weber, Max. 1976. 'Revolution? Counterrevolution? What Revolution?'. In W. Laqueur (ed) *Fascism: A Reader's Guide*, Berkeley, CA: University of California Press.

Weiss, Michael. 2017. 'Alt-right? Don't Be Afraid to Call Them Fascists'. *CNN*, August 15. https://edition.cnn.com/2017/08/14/opinions/fascism-and-its-name-michael-weiss-opinion/index.html

Weissman, Lavan. 1969. 'Introduction: Leon Trotsky's *Fascism: What It Is and How to Fight It*'. *marxists.org*. www.marxists.org /archive/trotsky/works/1944/1944-fas.htm

White, Gillian B. 2018. 'The Black and Hispanic Unemployment Rates Don't Deserve Applause'. *The Atlantic*, January 8. www.theatlantic.com/business/archive/2018/01/trump-black-hispanic-unemployment/549932/

Wikipedia. ongoing. 'Timeline of Protests Against Donald Trump'. https://en.m.wikipedia.org/wiki/Timeline_of_protests_against_Donald_Trump

Wilson, Jason. 2015. '"Cultural Marxism": A Uniting Theory for Rightwingers Who Love to Play the Victim'. *The Guardian*, January 19. www.theguardian.com/commentisfree/2015/jan/19/cultural-marxism-a-uniting-theory-for-right wingers-who-love-to-play-the-victim

Wolff, Michael. 2018a. *Fire and Fury: Inside the Trump White House*, New York, NY: Macmillan.

Wolff, Michael. 2018b. 'Interview on the Today Show'. *NBC*, January 5. www.clickondetroit.com/news/watch-full-today-show-interview-with-fire-and-fury-author-michael-wolff

Wolffe, Richard. 2017. 'Yet More Proof: Donald Trump Is a Fascist Sympathiser'. *The Guardian*, November 29. https://amp.theguardian.com/commentisfree/2017/nov/29/donald-trump-britain-first-fascist-sympathiser

Wood, Graeme. 2017. 'His Kampf'. *The Atlantic*, June. www.theatlantic.com/magazine/archive/2017/06/his-kampf/524505/

Workers World Party: What Is WWP? 2018. www.workers.org/wwp/what-is-wwp/

Zurcher, Anthony. 2018. 'Where Did Trump Haters Go?'. *BBC News US and Canada*, February 28. www.bbc.co.uk/news/world-us-canada-43220700

Index